Schema Therapy
for Borderline Personality
Disorder

Schema Therapy for Borderline Personality Disorder

Arnoud Arntz and Hannie van Genderen

Partly based on a Dutch first edition,
translated into English by Jolijn Drost,
Kyra Sendt, Stephanie Baumgarten-
Kustner and Arnoud Arntz.

A John Wiley & Sons, Ltd., Publication

This edition first published in English in 2009
English translation © 2009 John Wiley & Sons Ltd.
This book is a revised and extended version of: van Genderen, Hannie and Arntz, Arnoud
(2005) *Schemagerichte cognitieve therapie bij borderline persoonlijkheidsstoornis.* Amsterdam:
Uitgeverij Nieuwezijds

Wiley-Blackwell is an imprint of John Wiley & Sons, formed by the merger of Wiley's global
Scientific, Technical, and Medical business with Blackwell Publishing.

Registered Office
John Wiley & Sons Ltd, The Atrium, Southern Gate, Chichester, West Sussex, PO19 8SQ, UK

Editorial Offices
The Atrium, Southern Gate, Chichester, West Sussex, PO19 8SQ, UK
9600 Garsington Road, Oxford, OX4 2DQ, UK

350 Main Street, Malden, MA 02148-5020, USA

For details of our global editorial offices, for customer services, and for information about how
to apply for permission to reuse the copyright material in this book please see our website at
www.wiley.com/wiley-blackwell.

Library of Congress Cataloging-in-Publication Data

Arntz, Arnoud.
  Schema therapy for borderline personality disorders / Arnoud Arntz and Hannie van
Genderen.
    p. cm.
  Translated from the Dutch.
  Includes bibliographical references and index.
  ISBN 978-0-470-51080-3 (cloth) – ISBN 978-0-470-51081-0 (pbk.)   1. Borderline
personality disorders – Treatment.   2. Schema-focused cognitive therapy.   I. Genderen,
Hannie van.   II. Title.

  RC569.5.B67A76 2009
  616.85′852 – dc22

                                                                                    2008047077

British Library Cataloguing in Publication Data

A catalogue record for this book is available from the British Library

Typeset in 10.5/13 pt Minion by SNP Best-set Typesetter Ltd., Hong Kong

Printed in Singapore by Fabulous Printers Pte Ltd

Table of Contents

About the Authors

Arnoud Arntz, PhD, is a full professor of Clinical Psychology and Experimental Psychopathology at Maastricht University. He is Scientific Director of the University's Research Institute of Experimental Psychopathology and Director of the Postgraduate Clinical Psychology Programme in the south of the Netherlands. He is also associated as a psychotherapist with the Maastricht Community Mental Health Centre. He was project leader of the Dutch multi-centre trial comparing schema therapy with transference-focused psychotherapy. One of his main research interests is Borderline Personality Disorder (BPD).

Hannie van Genderen, MPhil, is Clinical Psychologist, Psychotherapist and Supervisor of the Dutch Association for Behavioural and Cognitive Therapy. She is a psychotherapist at the Maastricht Community Mental Health Centre and has been involved in the treatment of personality disorders for more than 15 years. She has taught cognitive behaviour therapy in postgraduate programmes for more than 20 years and has developed specialized courses in schema therapy for BPD and other personality disorders.

Preface

Schema therapy is a new integrative psychotherapy based on cognitive models, and offers an effective treatment of borderline personality disorder (BPD). A recent multi-centre trial conducted in the Netherlands demonstrated that schema therapy leads to recovery from BPD in about half of the patients, whereas two-thirds of the patients experience a clinically significant improvement (Giesen-Bloo *et al.*, 2006). Schema therapy proved to be more than twice as effective as a psychodynamic treatment in terms of recovery rates.

This book offers a practical guide for therapists to conduct schema therapy with BPD patients. Building upon Jeffrey Young's schema mode model, Young's schema therapy, and insights from Beck's and Arntz's cognitive therapy and experiential methods, it offers a conceptual model of BPD, a treatment model, and a wealth of methods and techniques for treating BPD patients. The treatment not only addresses the DSM BPD criteria-related problems, but also the psychopathological personality features underlying the symptoms, like attachment problems, punitive conscience, inadequately processed childhood traumas and so on. Research has demonstrated that patients improve in all these aspects, including on the level of automatic information processing.

The authors equate their treatment to blind simultaneous chess playing in a pinball machine, meaning that the therapist has to be actively aware of the abundance of quickly changing factors that play a role in the patient's problems, and simultaneously has to address them. Though treatment of BPD is complicated, many therapists can learn this method. Experienced therapists with good stamina will feel supported and stimulated by the book's practical explanations and examples. Central in the therapeutic relationship is the concept of 'limited reparenting', which forms the basis for a warm and collaborative relationship. A good therapeutic relationship is not enough, however. Therefore, numerous experiential, interpersonal, cognitive and behavioural methods and techniques are described that are specifically suited for the treatment of BPD patients. Finally, the book offers specific methods to be used in the treatment of very difficult cases and helps the therapist to deal with the many pitfalls that can arise from the treatment of BPD.

Acknowledgements

The writing of a book combined with a busy job at the Maastricht Community Mental Health Centre demanded much time, which I managed to find thanks to the unconditional support of my husband Leo Scheffer. He not only took over much of the care of the family but also helped me with reading and typing out the texts. I thank my children Sacha and Zoë for their patience as they heard 'not now' many times during this period.

I learned the treatment of patients with personality disorders thanks to the many training opportunities organized by Arnoud Arntz from the Maastricht University, by inviting, amongst others, Tim Beck, Cory Newman, Jeffrey Young, Christine Padesky and Kathleen Mooney. However, I especially learned a great deal from Arnoud himself, through his enthusiasm and assertiveness in continuously discovering new ways to treat 'untreatable' patients, just like the ones with borderline personality disorder.

I would like to thank my colleagues from the RIAGG Maastricht, particularly Arnoud Arntz, Tonny van Gisbergen, and Wiesette Krol from the Borderline peer supervision group, for their collaboration and support while learning to treat patients with borderline personality disorder. Marjon Nadort I want to thank for years of collaboration: with her I have given the majority of courses and workshops. Together we have always found better ways to teach schema therapy to colleagues.

I am also indebted to my colleagues Monique Wijers, Monique Auerbach, Ina Krijgsman and my brother-in-law Igor van de Wal as they have read the whole book, asked wise questions and suggested additions.

The patients I have treated may have contributed most to this book. Examples in this book are (anonymously) taken from our conversations, and I have learned a lot from them. The diagnosis of borderline personality disorder is unfortunately not yet accepted to the extent that I could list their names here. But my heartfelt thanks to you.

Hannie van Genderen

Without my teachers, one of them the co-author of this book, I should have never reached the point of treating people with borderline personality disorder. I am very grateful for this. I would like to give my special thanks to Tim Beck, Christine Padesky, Kathleen Mooney, Cory Newman and particularly Jeffrey Young for what they taught our team in their workshops. Jeffrey Young in particular deserves my thanks, as he developed a model that not only matched with my own early thinking about borderline personality disorder, but also developed a comprehensive treatment, which is the subject of this book. My therapist and research colleagues, amongst whom are the PhD candidates Laura Dreessen, Anoek Weertman, Simkje Sieswerda, Josephine Giesen-Bloo, Thea van Asselt and Jill Lobbestael, I also want to thank for the help they provided with developing the treatments and the research into borderline personality disorder. Moreover, I would like to thank the research assistants and interns who have conducted many studies, and especially the patients who have taken part in the treatment and the research, without whom we could not have gained insight into these complex problems and their treatment.

Ultimately, this book could not have come about without the opportunities offered by the Maastricht Community Mental Health Centre to the academic project of the Research Institute of Experimental Psychopathology of the Maastricht University, as well as the subsidies by the Dutch National Fund for Mental Health and the Fund for Developmental Medicine by the College for Care Insurances. Their grants enabled the training of the therapists for the multi-centre trial into treatments of borderline personality disorder and the conducting of this study, which empirically tested the effectiveness and cost-effectiveness of the treatment outlined in this book.

Thanks are due to Kyra Sendt and Jolijn Drost for their help with translating the original Dutch book into English.

Arnoud Arntz

Introduction

Until recently, patients with borderline personality disorder (BPD) were known as particularly difficult patients. They were viewed as patients who either could not be helped by therapy or, in the best-case scenario, showed low success rates to treatment. Meanwhile, their demands on both medical and mental health care are great and their dropout rates from treatment programmes are high.

In this book we describe a treatment for patients with BPD, which, in most cases, leads to recovery from this disorder or substantial clinical improvement. Schema therapy (ST) not only leads to a reduction in BPD symptoms, but also to lasting changes in the patient's personality.

In Chapter 1, BPD is defined and described, followed by a discussion of the development of this disorder.

Chapter 2 gives an explanation of ST, developed by Jeffrey Young, for BPD. This is the so-called schema mode model. The different schema modes for patients with BPD are described in this chapter.

In Chapter 3 we explain the aims and different phases of the therapy. Chapters 4 to 8 discuss different treatment methods and techniques. Chapter 4 involves seeing the therapeutic relationship as an instrument of change. Also the essential concept of 'limited reparenting', a central point of ST, is discussed at length.

Chapter 5 describes experiential techniques which are directed to changing the patients' perceptions. These techniques are; imagery rescripting; role playing, the two-or-more-chair technique; and experiencing and expressing feelings.

Schema Therapy for Borderline Personality Disorder. Arnoud Arntz and Hannie van Genderen
© 2009 John Wiley & Sons, Ltd.

The cognitive techniques used in this book are described and explained in Chapter 6. As there is a great deal of literature about these techniques, they are only briefly defined. This is also the case for the behavioural techniques described in Chapter 7.

Chapter 8 deals with a number of specific therapeutic methods and techniques. While these are not relevant for all BPD patients, they can be important and useful to the therapeutic setting.

Chapter 9 combines the previously described methods and techniques with the schema modes. The chapter explains which techniques are the most appropriate to each schema mode. The art of addressing different modes in a single session is also discussed in this chapter.

Chapter 10 deals with the final phase of therapy during which the patient no longer has BPD, but perhaps retains some of the personality characteristics and/or coping strategies, which could stand in the way of further positive changes.

Considering that a large percentage of BPD patients are female, the authors refer to the patient in the feminine form. Although many therapists are female, for the sake of clarity the authors refer to the therapist using the masculine form.

1

Borderline Personality Disorder

What is Borderline Personality Disorder?

Patients with borderline personality disorder (BPD) have problems with almost every aspect of their lives. They have problems with constantly changing moods, their relationships with others, unclear identities and impulsive behaviours. Outbursts of rage and crises are commonplace. Despite the fact that many BPD patients are intelligent and creative, they seldom succeed in developing their talents. Often their education is incomplete and they remain unemployed. If they work, it is often at a level far below their capabilities. They are at a great risk of self-harm by means of self-mutilation and/or substance abuse. The suicide risk is high and approximately 10% die as a result of a suicide attempt (Paris, 1993).

The DSM-IV diagnostic criteria for BPD are used as the standard definition for the diagnosis and indication of BPD and not the psychoanalytical definition of the borderline personality organization (Kernberg, 1976, 1996; Kernberg *et al.*, 1989). The borderline personality organization includes a number of personality disorders and axis-I disorders and is therefore far too extensive for the specific treatment for BPD that will be described here. According to the DSM-IV, patients must satisfy at least five of the nine criteria, as listed in Table 1.1, to obtain a diagnosis of BPD. The essential general feature of the DSM-IV definition of BPD is *instability* and its influence on the areas of interpersonal relationships, self-image, feelings and impulsiveness.

Schema Therapy for Borderline Personality Disorder. Arnoud Arntz and Hannie van Genderen
© 2009 John Wiley & Sons, Ltd.

Table 1.1   DSM-IV diagnostic criteria for borderline personality disorder.

A pervasive pattern of instability of interpersonal relationships, self-image and affects, as well as marked impulsivity, beginning by early adulthood and present in a variety of contexts, as indicated by at least five (or more) of the following criteria:

1. Frantic efforts to avoid real or imagined abandonment. Note: Not including suicidal or self-mutilating behaviour as covered in criterion 5.
2. A pattern of unstable and intense interpersonal relationships characterized by alternating between extremes of idealization and devaluation.
3. Identity disturbance: markedly and persistently unstable self-image or sense of self.
4. Impulsivity in at least two areas that are potentially self-damaging (e.g. spending, promiscuous sex, binge eating, substance abuse and reckless driving). Note: Not including suicidal or self-mutilating behaviour as covered in criterion 5.
5. Recurrent suicidal behaviour, gestures, threats or self-mutilating behaviour such as cutting, interfering with the healing of scars or picking at oneself.
6. Affective instability due to a marked reactivity of mood (e.g. intense episodic dysphoria, irritability or anxiety usually lasting a few hours and only rarely more than a few days).
7. Chronic feelings of emptiness, worthlessness.
8. Inappropriate anger or difficulty controlling anger (e.g. frequent displays of temper, constant anger and recurrent physical fights).
9. Transient, stress-related paranoid suicidal ideation or severe dissociative symptoms.

Source: APA (2000) DSM-IV-Tr.

Prevalence and Comorbidity

BPD is one of the most common mental disorders within the (outpatient) clinical population. Prevalence in the general population is estimated at 1.1% to 2.5% and varies in clinical populations depending on the setting, from 10% of the outpatients up to 20–50% of psychiatric committed patients. However, in many cases the diagnosis of BPD is still made late in assessment or not given at all. This might be due to the high comorbidity and other problems associated with BPD, which complicate the diagnostic process.

The comorbidity in this group of patients is high and diverse. On axis-I, there is often depression, eating disorders, social phobia, PTSD or relationship problems. In fact one can expect any or all of these disorders in stronger or weaker forms along with BPD.

All of the personality disorders can be co-morbid to BPD. A common combination is that of BPD along with narcissistic, antisocial, histrionic, paranoid, dependent and avoidant personality disorders (Layden *et al.*, 1993).

Reviews and studies by Dreessen and Arntz (1998), Mulder (2002) and Weertman *et al.* (2005) have shown that anxiety and mood disorders are treatable when the patient has a comorbidity with a personality disorder. However, in the case of BPD, one must be careful to only treat the axis-I disorder. BPD is a serious disorder that results in permanent disturbance of the patient's life with numerous crises and suicide attempts, which makes the usual treatment of axis-I disorders burdensome. Axis-I complaints and symptoms often change in nature and scope, making the diagnostic process even more difficult. This often results in the treating of BPD taking priority. Disorders that should take priority over BPD in treatment are described in '(Contra-) Indications' (see Chapter 2).

Development of BPD

The majority of patients with BPD have experienced sexual, physical and/ or emotional abuse in their childhood, in particular between the ages of 6 and 12 (Herman, Perry and van der Kolk, 1989; Ogata *et al.*, 1990; Weaver and Clum, 1993). It is more problematic to identify emotional abuse in BPD patients than to identify sexual or physical abuse. Emotional abuse often remains hidden or not acknowledged by the BPD patient out of a sense of loyalty towards the parents or due to a lack of knowledge of what a normal, healthy childhood involves.

These traumatic experiences in combination with temperament, insecure attachment, developmental stage of the child, as well as the social situation in which things took place, result in the development of dysfunctional interpretations of the patient's self and others (Arntz, 2004; Zanarini, 2000). Patients with BPD have a disorganized attachment style. This is the result of the unsolvable situation they experienced as a child, in which their parent was both a menace or threat, as well as a potential safe haven (van

IJzendoorn, Schuengel and Bakermans-Kranenburg, 1999). Translated into cognitive terms, a combination of dysfunctional schemas and coping strategies results in BPD (e.g. Arntz, 2004).

Patients with BPD have a very serious and complex set of problems. Because the patient's behaviour is so unpredictable, it exhausts the sympathy and endurance of family and friends. Life is not only difficult for the patients, but also for those around them. At times, life is so difficult that the patient gives up (suicide) or her support system gives up and breaks off contact with the patient. Treating BPD patients is also fatiguing for the mental health care giver.

Schema therapy offers BPD patients and therapists a treatment model in which the patient is helped to break through the dysfunctional patterns she has created and to achieve a healthier life.

2

Schema Therapy for Borderline Personality Disorder

The Development of Schema Therapy for Borderline Personality Disorder

Before the development of schema therapy (ST), BPD, as with many psychological disorders, was treated primarily from a psychoanalytical perspective. This started to change in the 1990s when cognitive behaviourists began to study the treatment of personality disorders with cognitive behavioural therapy.

The use of cognitive therapy for treating personality disorders was first introduced by Aaron Beck, Arthur Freeman and colleagues in their work *Cognitive Therapy of Personality Disorders* (1990). This new form of therapy achieved high success rates particularly in the reduction of symptoms such as suicidal behaviour (Beck, 2002). However, there was more limited success with deeper personality changes.

In that same year, Jeffrey Young introduced a new form of cognitive therapy, which he referred to as 'Schema-Focused Therapy', later 'Schema Therapy'. He later expanded upon this therapeutic model with the introduction of schema modes. His theory is based upon a combination of cognitive behavioural therapy and experiential techniques. There is a strong emphasis on the therapeutic relationship as a means of behavioural change, as well as on the emotional processing of traumatic experiences.

To date, ST appears to be a good method to achieve substantial personality improvements in BPD patients.

Schema Therapy for Borderline Personality Disorder. Arnoud Arntz and Hannie van Genderen
© 2009 John Wiley & Sons, Ltd.

Research Results

Research on traditional psychoanalytical forms of treatment showed high dropout percentages (46%–67%) and a relatively high percentage of suicide. Across four longitudinal studies, approximately 10% of the patients died during treatment or within 15 years following treatment due to suicide (Paris, 1993). This percentage is comparable to that of non-psychotherapeutically treated BPD patients (8–9%: as reported by Adams, Bernat and Luscher, 2001).

The first controlled study of cognitive behavioural treatment for BPD was realized by Linehan *et al.* (1991). The dialectical behavioural therapy they introduced had lower dropout rates, fewer hospitalizations, and a greater reduction in self-injury and suicidal behaviour in comparison with usual treatment. On other measurements of psychopathology, there were no significant differences when compared with control treatments. Uncontrolled studies as to the effectiveness of Beck's cognitive therapy also showed a reduction in suicide risk and depressive symptoms, as well as a decrease in the number of BPD symptoms (Arntz, 1999; Beck, 2002; Brown *et al.*, 2004). Moreover, the dropout rates during the first year were lower than normal (about 9%).

ST as developed by Young was recently studied in the Netherlands, where it was compared to Transference-Focused Psychotherapy (TFP), a psychodynamic method from Kernberg and co-workers (Giesen-Bloo *et al.*, 2006). This study started in 2000 and involved three years of treatment. ST showed more positive results than TFP in reduction of BPD symptoms, as well as other aspects of psychopathology and quality of life. In the follow-up study, four years after the start of the treatment, 52% of the patients who started ST recovered from BPD, while more than two-thirds showed clinically significant improvement in reducing BPD symptoms. These percentages are impressive given that dropouts (even those due to somatic illness) were included in the study.

One of the most compelling results from these studies is that *all* BPD problems were reduced and not only conspicuous symptoms such as self-harm. Furthermore, the patient's quality of life as a whole and her feeling of self-esteem were significantly improved. As a result of treatment, all psychopathological characteristics of BPD, whether symptomatic or personality related, were significantly improved. Similar results were found in a Norwegian series of case studies. When patients were measured post-treatment, 50% no longer met the criteria for BPD and 80% appeared to have notably profited from the treatment (Nordahl and Nysæter, 2005).

ST is an involved undertaking with a duration of approximately one and a half to four years (although longer may also prove necessary) and begins with two sessions a week (this can eventually be reduced to one session a week at a later stage). Despite the high treatment costs, there are indications that ST is cost-effective, as evidenced by a cost-effectiveness analysis showing that ST is not only superior to TFP in effects, but also less costly. Moreover, compared with baseline, ST leads to a reduction of societal costs for BPD patients, so that the net effect was a reduction of costs, despite the expense involved in delivery of ST (van Asselt *et al.*, 2008). Thus, given these positive results and the large BPD population, it seems a good idea to introduce the use of ST to a wider audience.

(Contra-) Indications

There are certain disorders that can complicate the diagnosis of BPD, in particular bipolar disorder, psychosis (this refers to psychotic disorder, not a short-term and reactive psychotic episode, which often occurs in BPD patients) and ADHD. The presence of these disorders complicates not only the diagnosis, but also interferes with treating BPD. Only after these disorders are dealt with it is possible to focus on treating BPD.

In the case of a comorbidity of disorders, specific disorders must be addressed before ST can be considered for BPD. These are severe major depression, severe substance abuse in need of clinical detoxification and anorexia nervosa. The seriousness of these disorders will act as contraindications for the use of ST for BPD. In addition, developmental disorders such as autism or Asperger's syndrome are problematic for ST. ST assumes that while development may be disturbed or delayed, it is not neurologically abnormal. Thus, abnormal neurological development may also interfere with the use of ST.

In the study by Giesen-Bloo *et al.* (2006), antisocial personality disorder was also excluded from this treatment. This was insisted upon by the TFP experts. However, pilot studies using ST with antisocial personality disorder have shown positive results indicating ST may be a possible form of treatment for these patients.

Rationale of Treatment/Theories Supporting Treatment

ST as described by Young states that everyone develops schemas during childhood. A schema is an organized knowledge structure, which develops during childhood and manifests in certain behaviours, feelings and thoughts (Arntz and Kuipers, 1998). While a schema is not directly measurable, it can be gauged by analysing the patient's life history and observing the manner in which she deals with her temperament and talents. This becomes more evident and observable as the patient shares more details about her behaviour in various social situations and the life rules and strategies to which she adheres.

Healthy schemas develop when the basic needs of a child are met. This enables children to develop positive images about other individuals, themselves and the world as a whole.

The basic needs of children include:

Safety – Children must be able to depend on a reliable adult for care and a safe place to live, develop and grow.

Connection to others – Children must feel that they are connected to others and are able to share their experiences, thoughts and feelings with others.

Autonomy – Children must have a safe and secure environment from where they can explore and learn about the world. The ultimate goal of maturing to adulthood is for them to eventually stand on their own two feet. Caregivers must slowly but surely allow children to separate from them in order to grow into autonomous adults.

Self-appreciation – Children must have an adequate sense of appreciation. In order to develop a strong sense of self-esteem, they must be appreciated for who they are as people and what they are capable of doing.

Self-expression – The expression of one's opinions and feelings must be learnt and stimulated without being held back by strict or oppressive rules.

Realistic limits – In order to live in a society with others, it is necessary for children to learn certain rules. They must understand when to subdue their autonomy or self-expression when dealing with others and be capable of doing so. Children also have to learn to tolerate and adequately deal with frustrations (Young and Klosko, 1994; Young, Klosko and Weishaar, 2003).

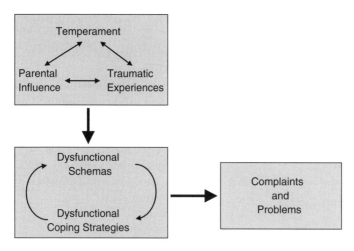

Figure 2.1   The development of dysfunctional schemas.

When these needs are not met, whether solely due to shortcomings in the child's background, or in combination with traumatic events (such as loss of a parent or sexual abuse), this can form – in interaction with the temperament of the child – dysfunctional schemas and coping strategies (see Figure 2.1). Young describes 18 different schemas (see Appendix I) and coping strategies (see Appendix J) (Young, Klosko and Weishaar, 2003).

The schemas, while not exactly the same as the personality disorders (as described in the DSM-IV; APA, 1994), can easily be compared to them (see Table 2.1).

Schema Modes

Patients with BPD often have so many different schemas present at the same time that both patient and therapist cannot see the wood for the trees. Because shifts in behaviour and feelings take place so quickly, it is difficult for the patient herself, let alone for those around her, to understand what is taking place. This further exacerbates an already complex problem. These sudden shifts in patterns of feeling, thinking and behaviour, which are so common in BPD, have inspired the development of the concept 'schema modes' (also called 'modus' or 'schema states') (McGinn and Young, 1996). A schema mode is a set of schemas and processes, which, in certain

Table 2.1   The relationship between DSM-IV personality disorders and schemas.

Personality disorder	Schemas
Paranoid	Mistrust/abuse
	Emotional deprivation
	Social isolation/alienation
Schizoid	Social isolation/alienation
Schizotypal	Mistrust/abuse
	Social isolation/alienation
	Vulnerability to harm or illness
Antisocial	Abandonment/instability
	Mistrust/abuse
	Emotional deprivation
	Entitlement
	Insufficient self-control/self-discipline
Borderline	Abandonment/instability
	Mistrust/abuse
	Emotional deprivation
	Defectiveness/shame
	Dependence/incompetence
	Vulnerability to harm or illness
	Insufficient self-control/self-discipline
	Subjugation
	Emotional inhibition
	Punitiveness
Histrionic	Abandonment/instability
	Emotional deprivation
	Entitlement
	Insufficient self-control/self-discipline
Narcissistic	Entitlement
	Insufficient self-control/self-discipline
	Defectiveness/shame
Avoidant	Social isolation/alienation
	Social undesirability
	Defectiveness/shame
	Failure
	Subjugation
Dependent	Dependence/incompetence
	Abandonment/instability
	Defectiveness/shame
	Subjugation

Table 2.1 *Continued*

Personality disorder	Schemas
Obsessive-compulsive	Unrelenting standards/hypercriticalness
	Emotional inhibition
Passive-aggressive	Failure
	Mistrust/abuse
Depressive	Mistrust/abuse
	Defectiveness/shame
	Social isolation/alienation
	Social undesirability
	Vulnerability to harm or illness
	Failure
	Subjugation

Adapted from Sprey (2002).

situations, override the thoughts, feelings and actions of the patient at the cost of other schemas. In other words, when the BPD patient is relatively relaxed and comfortable, one sees a totally different side of her personality as opposed to when she feels threatened. Under normal circumstances, one sees a relatively relaxed patient who appears to have few emotions. However, when, for example, the threat of abandonment by an important figure is posed, one then sees a 'young child' being very upset and completely inconsolable. A patient with BPD can switch from one strong mood or emotion to another in a very short period of time. According to the schema mode model, this is due to the patient's continual and uncontrolled shifts from one mode to the other.

Young suggested that the following five modes are characteristic of BPD: the detached protector, the abandoned/abused child, the angry/impulsive child, the punitive parent and the healthy adult. These modes can be renamed to make them more applicable to the patient's situation (see Figure 2.2). We must strongly emphasize that this heuristic model does not infer that BPD is a multiple personality disorder. Giving names to the different modes is a means of helping the patient to better understand and identify with the mode and does not have any reference to identities or persons (Arntz and Kuipers, 1998).

The following are descriptions of the different modes most prominent in BPD. Chapter 9 further describes treatment and how therapists can best address the different modes.

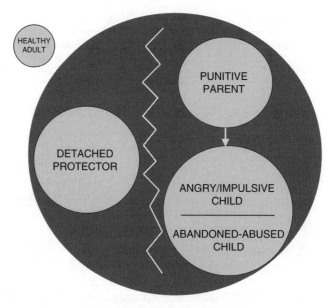

Figure 2.2   Borderline personality disorder: five modes (based on Arntz and Bögels, 2000).

The detached protector

When the patient is in the detached protector mode, the patient seems relatively mature and calm. A therapist could assume the patient is doing well. In fact, the patient uses this protective mode in order to avoid experiencing or revealing her feelings of fear (abandoned child), inferiority (punishing parent) or anger (impulsive child). Underlying assumptions that play important roles here are those of: it is dangerous to show your feelings and/or desires and to express your opinion. The patient fears losing control of her feelings. She attempts to protect herself from the alleged abuse or abandonment. This becomes particularly evident as she becomes attached to others. The protector keeps other people at a distance either by not engaging in contact or by pushing them away. Should others discover her weaknesses, the patient would face potential humiliation, punishment and/or abandonment. Therefore, for her it is better to not feel anything at all and keep others from getting too close to her.

Sample dialogue with a patient in the protector mode

(In this example and following dialogues, 'T' is therapist and 'P' is patient.)

T: How are you doing?
P: (with no emotion) Good.
T: How was your week, did anything happen that you would like to talk about?
P: (looks away and yawns) No, not really.
T: So, everything's OK?
P: Yeah, everything's OK. Maybe we could have a short session today?

Should simple methods of avoiding painful emotions prove ineffective, she may attempt other manners of escape, such as substance abuse, self-injury (physical pain can sometimes numb psychological pain), staying in bed, disassociation or attempting to end her life. BPD patients often describe this mode as an empty space or a cold feeling. They report feeling distanced from all experiences while in this mode, including therapy.

If the patient is not successful at keeping people at a distance, she can become angry and cynical in an attempt to keep people away from her. It is important for the therapist to recognize these behaviours as forms of protection and not be put off by them. If this angry state is very pronounced, it can be distinguished as a separate 'angry protector' mode.

It is difficult to distinguish the angry protector from the punitive parent, especially during the initial stages of the therapy. One manner of distinction is to observe the direction of the patient's anger. While the angry protector's rage is directed towards the therapist (or someone else), the punitive parent's anger is directed towards the patient herself. If the therapist is unsure of the mode he is presented with, he can simply ask the patient if she is able to disclose which 'side' of her personality is currently active.

Sample dialogue with patient in the angry protector and the punitive parent mode

T: When I told you that I have the next few days off, your reaction was pretty angry. What mode do you think that reaction came from?

Response from angry protector:

P: Oh No! We're going to have another lecture about that stupid border-line model of yours? You couldn't wait, could you? Can't think of anything better can you?

Response from punitive parent:

P: I don't know which 'side' of me this is. I only know that I must have been a complete idiot to trust you and that is one mistake I won't make again. It doesn't matter anyway, I'll never get better.

In the beginning of the therapy, the subtle differences between the angry protector and the angry child can also be difficult to distinguish. The differences are primarily evident in the level of anger that is paired with the reaction (see the section 'Angry/Impulsive Child').

These examples involve the protector expressing herself in a demonstrable, interactive manner. The completely opposite form in which the protector may express herself is by exhibiting tired or sleepy behaviour. In this case the therapist must assess whether or not the patient is actually tired or whether she is in the protector mode.

There is the risk that while in the protector mode, the patient may avoid therapy and not work on her problems with a serious chance of her stopping therapy all together. The patient can also have problems with dissociative symptoms, self-injury, addiction to numbing substances (e.g. drugs or alcohol) or may attempt suicide. Because of this, it is important to identify when the protector role is present and circumvent it. This will give the patient an opportunity to work on her actual problems.

The abandoned/abused child

The abandoned and/or abused child is often referred to as 'Little ...' (= the name of the patient). In our examples, we refer to the patient as Nora. Therefore, when in this mode she becomes 'Little Nora'.

Little Nora is sad, desperate, inconsolable and often in complete panic. When in this mode the patient's voice itself often changes to that of a child. Her thoughts and behaviour become that of a four- to six-year-old. She feels alone in the world and is convinced that no one cares about her. The basic belief in this mode is that she can trust no one. Everyone will abuse her and eventually abandon her. The world is a threatening, dangerous place that holds no future for her. Little Nora thinks in terms of black and white. She demands constant and immediate reassurance and solutions to her problems. She is incapable of helping herself. There is a great chance that during the first phase of the therapy, the therapist will face Little Nora mainly in situations of crisis. In the early stage of the therapeutic process, it is unlikely the patient will show her abandoned child side at other moments (for a sample dialogue, see Chapter 9, 'Treatment Methods for the Abandoned and Abused Child').

When the patient is in this mode, she latches onto the therapist in the hope that he holds the solutions to all of her problems. She expects complete and constant comfort and compassion from him. During this mode the therapist often feels overwhelmed by the patient's expectations of him. In an attempt to address her cries for help, he can have the tendency to look for practical solutions far too quickly. On the other hand, he may also attempt to rid himself of the patient by referring her to a crisis centre. When Nora is in a panic, all practical solutions appear unfeasible. Little Nora cannot comprehend that the crisis will ever come to an end.

Nora's feelings of desperation and the therapist's feelings of incompetence will only become greater if the therapist continues to advise practical solutions. Should she be referred on too quickly, Little Nora becomes even more desperate as she feels misunderstood and rejected.

The therapist must allow Little Nora's presence in these sessions. He must be supportive of her, validate her feelings, offer a safe haven, encourage her to bond with him as a therapist and address her past abuse. In short, he must offer her what she was most likely denied during her childhood.

The angry/impulsive child

The other child mode in BPD is that of the 'angry/impulsive child'. The beginning of therapy is often overshadowed by desperation (Little Nora) and shame (punitive parent). Because of this, one does not often see the angry/impulsive child in the beginning of the therapy.

Angry Nora is a furious, frustrated and impatient young child (approximately four years of age) who has no regard or consideration for others. When in this mode, the patient is often verbally and, at times, physically aggressive and acrimonious towards others including her therapist. She is incensed that her needs are not met and her rights go unacknowledged.

Angry Nora is convinced it is better to take all you can or you will end up with nothing at all. She is convinced she will be taken advantage of. She is not only furious, but also wants everyone to see just how badly she has been treated. She does this by attacking others (verbally or physically), hurting herself, attempting to kill herself, or even others, as a form of revenge. This, of course, is the extreme form of Angry Nora. A milder way in which Angry Nora may show the therapist her anger is by not attending sessions or stopping therapy all together.

While the differences between the angry child and the angry protector are not always clear, they can usually be observed in how the anger is presented. The angry child is impulsive and unreasonable. She refers to issues that are completely unrelated and irrelevant. The angry protector is more controlled and more likely to be cynical than furious (see Chapter 9 'Treatment Methods for the Angry/Impulsive Child' for a sample dialogue).

Outbursts of rage are impulsive and unexpected. Should these take place during a session, the therapist should attempt to remain calm and tolerate the anger. He should only limit the display of anger when the patient threatens to damage persons or property, or when the expression of her anger is so humiliating that the therapist feels his limits are violated.

The purpose of therapy is to teach the patient that she can be angry, but that there are other ways to express this emotion than the impulsive and extreme manner she currently adheres to.

A second characteristic of this mode is the impulsive way BPD patients try to get their needs met. The patient may, for instance, have sexual contacts with people she doesn't really know, in an attempt to get a feeling of being of value and cared for. Other examples are impulsive buying, impulsive alcohol or drug use, and impulsive eating. Such behaviours are related to this mode when they are impulsive (the patient did not really contemplate the long-term risks), often motivated by a sort of rebelliousness against the punitive mode, and have the aim of need satisfaction. Alcohol and benzodiazepine use, especially in combination, might lead to a loss of (the already problematic) inhibition of these kinds of impulses. The general aim of the treatment is that patients learn to acknowledge their needs (instead of trying to detach from them) and develop healthier ways of getting their needs met.

The punitive parent

The mode of the punitive parent usually also gets a name. When it is very clear which parent represents the punitive parent for the patient this mode can be given a name such as 'your punitive mother [father]'. Sometimes the patient may be unwilling or unable to actually give a name to the punitive parent out of a sense of misplaced loyalty towards that parent.

When this is the case, the patient can refer to her 'punishing side' or 'the punisher'.

The punitive parent is taunting in her manner and has a tone of disapproval and humiliation. She thinks that Nora is bad and deserves to be punished. The punitive parent states that Nora is showing off. When Nora fails, it is simply because she has not tried hard enough. Feelings are of little interest to the punitive parent and, according to this side, she uses them only to manipulate others. Should something go wrong, it is her own fault. In her mind, succeeding is dependent entirely upon her desire to succeed. If she really wants something, it will work out. If she fails or it does not work out, she obviously did not want it enough.

Sample dialogue with a patient in the punitive parent mode

T: How are you doing?
P: (in an angry voice) Bad.
T: Why is that, did something bad happen?
P: No, I did something stupid and now everything is ruined.
T: So things are not going well with you?
P: No, I'm hopeless and now I'm bothering you as well.

When the punitive parent is present, Little Nora cowers away and is difficult to reach.

While in this mode, the patient will punish herself by purposely denying herself enjoyable things or by ruining them. She will also punish herself by hurting herself or attempting to end her life. She provokes punishment everywhere, even from her therapist. She refuses to aid in her own recovery by spurning activities that would promote healthy improvement. This often results in a premature end to the therapy.

When the patient is in this mode, the objective of the therapy involves extinguishing the unhealthy rules and behaviours and replacing them with more adequate rules and norms.

The healthy adult

It may seem odd to have a 'healthy adult' mode when dealing with BPD, but it is exactly this mode that the patient needs to cultivate and eventually maintain. Due to absence of a normal, healthy childhood, as well as uncontrollable events during this period, the healthy adult mode is seldom strongly present during the initial stages of the therapy.

The patient's deficit of healthy development in areas such as bonding with others, autonomy, self-expression, self-value and the lack of experience in dealing with realistic limitations, requires the therapist to serve as a representative of the 'healthy side' particularly in the beginning of the therapy.

However, it is the healthy adult who initially ensures that the patient seeks out and remains in therapy. At later stages of therapy this mode helps the patient to achieve healthy goals. These therapeutic goals such as relationships with others, looking for educational or work opportunities, and other such activities that the patient will enjoy and be capable of completing, are necessary for successful completion of the therapeutic process. While in this mode the patient not only dares to show her feelings, but also shows she is capable of controlling their expression, a necessary skill for the BPD patient to accomplish.

As previously stated, in the beginning of the therapy, it is the therapist who serves as a representative of the so-called healthy side. By the end of the therapy, the healthy adult is so evolved that she can take this role over from the therapist and the therapy can be concluded in a healthy, appropriate manner.

Summary

There is a saying that necessity is the mother of invention. ST was developed out of necessity. It was necessary to expand upon cognitive techniques as these therapies were not helpful enough in treating personality problems. By adjusting techniques from other therapy schools and fitting them into a cognitive framework, a new form of integrated therapy was created: 'Schema Therapy'. The first research results indicate that ST is an effective and cost-effective treatment of BPD.

The schema mode model attempts to give insight as to why patients with BPD have such strong mood changes and erratic behaviours. We will now continue with a description of the different phases of therapy (Chapter 3), and the most important techniques (Chapters 5–8). We will then return to schema modes in Chapter 9, to explain how different techniques can be applied for the different modes in the different phases of treatment.

3

Treatment

The process of change is approached along three distinct pathways when treating BPD: feeling, thinking and doing. These pathways correspond to the three levels of knowledge representation that are present in the schemas: explicit knowledge (thinking), implicit 'felt' knowledge (including emotional representations or feeling) and operational representations (doing).

In addition to these three pathways, we can also distinguish three differ-ent topics, which can be addressed by these pathways. These topics are life outside of therapy, experiences in therapy and past experiences. The path-ways and topics are presented in a matrix in Table 3.1 so that it is clear which relevant therapeutic techniques can be best applied during any of the given situations.

Whatever topic the patient focuses on and whatever pathway is tried, these techniques can only be successful once a certain level of trust and attachment to the therapist is formed (see 'within therapy' in Table 3.1). Because of the importance of the relationship between patient and thera-pist, we will address this relationship in Chapter 4 immediately after dis-cussing treatment in this chapter. Only once this relationship is fully addressed will we move on to the techniques. First we will discuss the change of implicit knowledge in Chapter 5 (experiential techniques), then thinking or explicit knowledge in Chapter 6 (cognitive techniques) and finally 'doing' or changing operational representation in Chapter 7 (behav-ioural techniques). All of the subjects found in the matrix (Table 3.1) can be found in the following chapters. However, first we will examine the phases involved in the course of treating BPD with ST.

Schema Therapy for Borderline Personality Disorder. Arnoud Arntz and Hannie van Genderen
© 2009 John Wiley & Sons, Ltd.

Table 3.1   Therapeutic techniques.

Focus	Channel		
	Feeling	*Thinking*	*Doing*
Outside therapy	*Role-plays present situations *Imagining present situations *Practise feeling emotions *Exposure to showing emotions	*Socratic questioning *Formulating new schemas *Schema dialogue *Flashcards *Positive logbook	*Behavioural experiments *Role playing skills *Problem solving *Trying out new behaviour
Within therapy	*Limited reparenting *Empathic confrontation *Setting limits *Role switching therapist/patient	*Recognizing patient's schemas in the therapeutic relationship *Challenging ideas about therapist *Recognizing therapist's schemas *Self-disclosure	*Behavioural experiments *Strengthening functional behaviour *Training skills related to the therapeutic relationship *Modelling by therapist
Past	*Imagery rescripting *Role-plays past *Two-or-more-chair technique *Writing letters	*Reinterpretation of past events and integration into new schemas *Historical test	*Testing of new behaviours on key individuals from the past

Structure of Treatment

Treatment begins with a comprehensive inventory of the problems as the patient experiences them. This is done in connection with a thorough explanation of the schema mode model. Also included in these beginning sessions is a discussion of practical matters such as the frequency of sessions (once or twice a week) and the expected duration of the therapy (one-and-a-half to four years or longer if necessary).

The recording of therapeutic sessions is not unusual. What is unique to ST is that the patient is given this recording and asked to listen to it before the next session takes place. Listening to the recorded sessions strengthens the effect of the therapy. No one is capable of incorporating all the information involved in a single session. Therefore, it is a very beneficial tool for the patient to listen to the recorded session. Often it is only upon listening to the recording that a patient actually hears and comprehends what was said during the session. During the actual session the patient could be in a mode that is not conducive to listening or processing information. Modes can distort how tone and language are perceived and therefore strongly influence information processing. Because of this, listening or re-listening, to recorded sessions not only reiterates the session itself, it also serves as proof of what was actually said and done during the session.

Sample of listening to a recorded session

Nora stated more and more often that she experienced my questions during sessions about something that had taken place as punishing. She thought that what I really wanted to say was that she had made a mistake and that the resulting consequences were her own fault. She was in the punishing mode. It was only when she later listened to the recording while in a young child mode or a healthy adult mode that she was able to actually hear my tone and realized that I was simply interested in how things were going and was not judging her.

Finally it is important that agreements are made regarding the therapist's availability. The patient needs clear guidelines as to when she can (and cannot) contact the therapist outside of sessions. She needs to know what courses of action to take when a crisis is approaching and to whom she can turn when the therapist is unavailable (see Chapter 4, 'Limited Reparenting'). Normally there is another member of the peer supervision group who is involved in the therapy from the sidelines. He can temporarily replace the therapist if needed, for example, in case of holidays or illness.

Phases in Treatment

Schema therapy (ST) for BPD patients does not have a fixed protocol that describes per session which issues need to be addressed. After all, this is a therapy that covers two to three years. There are, however, a number of distinguishable phases in the therapy, which will be described later. It is important to the protocol of ST that the therapist is aware of how best to react towards the different modes. Because of the importance of this we have chosen, after describing the separate therapeutic techniques (Chapters 5–8), to devote a chapter on how the therapist can deal with each mode during different phases of the therapy (Chapter 9). In Chapter 10 we will give separate attention to the final phase of the therapy.

While there is no set order to these phases, there are seven distinctive and distinguishable periods of therapy. Some phases may be omitted while others may recur at a later stage of therapy. These phases are:

1. starting phase and case conceptualization;
2. treating axis-I symptoms;
3. crisis management;
4. therapeutic interventions with schema modes;
5. treating childhood traumas;
6. changing behavioural patterns;
7. ending therapy.

Starting Phase and Case Conceptualization

The initial phase of the therapy involves approximately 6 to 12 sessions during which a complete diagnostic interview takes place. During this interview, all information relevant to the patient's problems and complaints is described in detail by the patient. A comprehensive anamnestic interview is conducted and the therapist begins to search for the relationship with parents/caregivers and possible events that are relevant to the formation of dysfunctional schemas. After this, the therapist looks into contraindications before continuing with treatment (see Chapter 2, '(Contra-) Indications') as well as measuring the patient's level of functioning and BPD symptoms. Together the therapist and patient create a case concept based upon the mode model (see Chapter 2). The different modes are described to the patient in terms she can understand and identify with (see Figure 3.1).

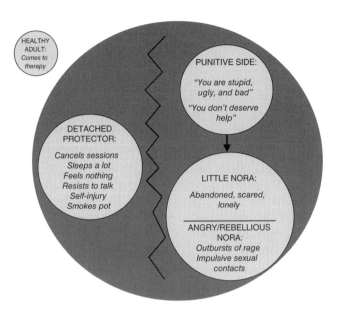

Figure 3.1 Case conceptualization Nora.

Further, the therapist works on developing a safe, healthy therapeutic relationship with the patient during this phase. This relationship is one of limited reparenting, a kind of restrained parenthood that involves the therapist offering the patient a great deal of security and support (see Chapter 4, 'Limited Reparenting').

The process of treating a BPD patient seldom begins with a calm conversation of information collection and case conceptualization. One should not be surprised when this process of information gathering is more of a rollercoaster as opposed to a quiet drive in the country. Often from day one it is clear that the patient is not comfortable or in a state to embark on a productive relationship with the therapist. The development of a therapeutic relationship and the gathering of information will be discussed in the following paragraphs.

Developing a relationship and gathering information

In order to make the patient feel safe and understood from the very first session, the therapist takes a friendly, open and not distanced position (see

Chapter 4, 'Limited Reparenting'). He spends a lot of time with the current problems of the patient and empathizes with her feelings. He examines, in conjunction with the patient, which situations trigger intense emotions. Further, he also looks at how she usually deals with her problems and in how far this is helpful in solving them. He informs himself about the patient's expectations towards the therapy and the therapist, and asks for previous experiences with therapy. Often the patient has already had experience with a number of different therapies, which produced limited results or even a damaging effect, for instance broken trust (sometimes even sexual abuse) of the patient through the therapist. Therefore, the therapist must be aware that the patient might distrust him in advance. He explains how far the patient's expectations can be met in the therapy and what the general rules are (see discussion in Chapter 4).

The patient's personal history is mapped and put into relation with the emergence of the schema modes. The therapist analyses which experiences in the past have contributed to the current problems. Here, it is possible to use a short imagery exercise to examine the link between the past and the present (see Chapter 5).

Measurements

To assess the patient's schemas, as well as explore influencing factors, the Young Schema Questionnaire (Young, 1999) and other questionnaires are completed by the patient after the first few sessions. The results are discussed with the patient. The Young Parenting Inventory can be helpful in clarifying factors that have influenced the development of the modes. The Borderline Personality Disorder Severity Index (BPDSI) is a structured interview that assesses the seriousness and frequency of BPD symptoms and expressions that meet DSM-IV criteria and have been experienced within the previous three-month period (Arntz *et al.*, 2003; Giesen-Bloo *et al.*, 2006, 2008).

With the help of the BPD checklist the patient can indicate to what extent her BPD symptoms have been a burden to her in the past month (Arntz and Dreessen, 1995; Giesen-Bloo *et al.*, 2008). The Personality Disorder Beliefs Questionnaire (PDBQ) includes a subscale with statements specifically relating to BPD (Arntz *et al.*, 2004). From the Personality Beliefs Questionnaire (PBQ) a series of items specific to BPD have been derived (Butler *et al.*, 2002). Recently the Schema Mode Inventory (SMI) and the

Young Atkinson Mode Inventory (YAMI) were developed, which can be helpful in clarifying the schema modes (Lobbestael *et al.*, 2008).

Explaining the treatment rationale

Once a diagnosis of BPD has been established, the therapist begins to explain the rationale behind the therapy by means of the BPD model and its modes. He explains how the patient's current problems are connected to schemas and modes. He further explains how each schema mode brings along with it certain feelings, thoughts and behaviours (see Appendix A: Schema therapy for patients). For a more in-depth explanation, the patient can refer to a number of relevant chapters in *Reinventing Your Life* (Young and Klosko, 1994).

Most BPD patients find the experience of learning about the Borderline model enlightening. It offers a clear explanation as to why they experience sudden mood swings and have so little control over their behaviour (see Chapter 9, 'A Simultaneous Chess Play in a Pinball Machine'). It also offers them the hope that change is possible and that they are not doomed to a life filled with uncontrolled behaviour and mood swings.

If the patient finds that this model is not appropriate to her situation, there are usually two possibilities: one is that the individual simply does not have BPD. The other possibility is that not only does the person have BPD but there is also a very strong protector mode at work. Because of this protector, everything the therapist says is considered to be dubious and unreliable. If the latter is the case, the therapist must take more time in building a trusting relationship with the patient and not dwell upon attempting to convince the patient of the schema model.

Treating Axis-I Symptoms

There are a number of symptoms that require primary attention before ST can begin. As described in the section on contraindications (Chapter 2), this involves a limited number of symptoms and disorders. In all other cases, this phase may be omitted. It is possible that these symptoms will arise at a later stage of therapy. In that case, it is necessary to return to this phase of therapy and deal with these issues. The treatment of these specific symptoms is not discussed in this book as their treatment does not differ for patients without BPD and can be found adequately explained in other works.

Crisis Management

Crisis management can be skipped when there is no crisis present at the beginning of the therapy. Apart from that, this can also be returned to later in the therapy. Should a crisis be present, it indeed requires the highest attention (see Chapter 8, 'Crisis').

Therapeutic Interventions with Schema Modes

This is the central phase of therapy and can have a duration of a number of years (see Chapters 5–10). The first phase of therapy is closed only when the patient can adequately explain how the schema modes work in her own words and the therapist has explained how he is going to set about the therapy (his working method). This is not to say that it is unnecessary to occasionally return to this point for a short 'refresher course' in the mode model at a later stage of treatment. However, at a certain point the therapist must stop gathering information and giving explanations and move on to changing thoughts and behaviours. Many therapists find this an uncomfortable point in the therapy. One could describe this moment as similar to the fear of diving off the deep end, particularly when starting with a new technique (e.g. the experiential techniques). Do not hesitate but simply jump in! Of course one can always turn to the peer supervision group and ask for advice.

Treating Childhood Traumas

In order to deal with childhood traumas, the patient must first bolster her healthy adult mode as well as develop and maintain supportive relationships outside of therapy. Because of this, dealing with childhood traumas usually does not take place until later stages of the therapy. This is not a stage of therapy one should omit, not even when the patient appears to be doing well, the trauma appears to be accepted or dealing with the trauma appears to be unnecessary (see Chapter 8, 'Trauma Processing').

Changing Behavioural Patterns

Young *et al.* (2003) referred to this phase of therapy as the longest and most crucial (see Chapter 10, 'Behavioural Pattern-Breaking'). Even when the patient is no longer ruled by constantly changing modes and the healthy adult has been developed, enacting upon these new behaviours is not always easy.

Ending Therapy

Closure to therapy is considered only when the patient no longer meets the criteria for a diagnosis of BPD, has built up a relatively stable social network and has found a meaningful way of filling her days (see Chapter 10, 'Ending Therapy') or when there is no progress after at least one year of ST.

4

The Therapeutic Relationship

Creating a safe, trusting relationship will take a lot of time, energy and commitment from the therapist as most BPD patients have a long history of relationships in which neglect, abuse and exploitation took place. It is sad to say but some of these negative experiences are regrettably with therapists or other health care professionals. Because of this, therapists must spend a great deal of time and energy in creating a safe, trusting therapeutic relationship with their patients. In addition, many patients have experienced relationships with therapists that were bad or had come to a premature end.

It is important for the therapist to have a great deal of patience as well as the support of a good peer supervision group. In comparison with other forms of psychotherapy, this treatment demands a great deal of both time and involvement. The therapist must, on the one hand, be unusually involved with his patient while at the same time maintaining the ability to set his own boundaries and in doing so protecting those of his patient. Therefore, the therapist has to be aware of his own (dysfunctional) schemas and must be able to deal with them in a healthy way. In the following paragraphs we illustrate important elements of the therapeutic relationship between the BPD patient and the therapist.

Limited Reparenting

Limited reparenting can be viewed as a form of constrained parenthood in which the therapist's demeanour forms the basis for the therapeutic process.

Schema Therapy for Borderline Personality Disorder. Arnoud Arntz and Hannie van Genderen
© 2009 John Wiley & Sons, Ltd.

In other words, the therapist goes into this relationship as if he were a parent figure for the patient. Please take note of the words 'as if'. It is not the intention of this therapy for the therapist to become the parent but rather help model appropriate parental behaviours and reactions. The therapist starts therapy with the understanding that he is prepared to invest at least three years (or more if necessary) in working with the patient. At times the therapist might have to invest extra time in the treatment of the patient, for example, when there is a crisis. When treating BPD patients we recommend that the therapist remains easily accessible to the patient. Therapists in the trial testing ST (Giesen-Bloo *et al.*, 2006) went so far as to provide their patients with telephone numbers where they could be reached outside office hours in cases of crisis or suicide attempts. If the therapist is able to personally accommodate the patient during a crisis, not only will this help to eleviate the crisis in a timely fashion, but it will also strengthen the relationship with the therapist. Upon completion of her therapy, Nora stated that simply knowing she was able to contact her therapist in the event of a crisis was very important to her. It gave her the feeling that she was valued and cared about. During her three years of therapy, Nora called her therapist 10 times outside office hours; 8 of these 10 times were during the first year. By providing a patient with a telephone number to use in the event of a crisis or suicide attempt, the therapist is not providing 24-hour care for his patient. The therapist is making himself available by means of, for example, a pager on which the patient can leave a message describing the seriousness of her situation. In this manner the therapist is on the one hand temporarily unavailable (e.g. at a concert/theatre, sleeping or away for the weekend), but, the message system provides the patient with immediate access to her therapist. For some patients simply hearing the therapist's voice on the answering machine offers enough reassurance to help them through whatever crisis is at hand. If there is an acute crisis requiring immediate attention and the therapist is not available, the patient can follow the protocol discussed during the first sessions. This will require her to turn to others for help such as her primary physician or a crisis centre.

Limited parenthood implies that the therapist fosters the neglected components of the patient's past. He offers direction when the patient is incapable of addressing a problem and sets limits when necessary. The therapist will work with her in developing and improving her abilities and encouraging her to develop her autonomy and responsibility. In time, the patient will internalize the role the therapist plays by building healthier schemas, which will in turn help her to build a new life. The different elements that are involved in limited reparenting are described in the following paragraphs.

Good care

The therapist must be able to offer more than the average amount of involvement when dealing with a BPD patient. Further, he must be prepared to continue this care for a long period of time. As with every parent–child relationship, this will not always be easy or pleasant for the patient. This is often further exasperated by the expectations of the patient. Because her basic needs were not met during her childhood, BPD patients tend to have high expectations of their therapists. Therefore, the therapist must have a clear idea as to what he will and will not do for the patient and he must communicate these limits in a clear way (see the section 'Setting Limits'). The manner in which this is done differs between therapists and is a regular subject during peer supervision meetings. Therapists who have this above-average willingness to make the extra effort with this rather demanding therapy, often have the tendency to exceed their own limitations (or allow their limits to be broken) too long before setting limits. At these moments there is an increased risk of burnout or boundary-exceeding behaviour like starting a non-therapeutic relationship with the patient. The therapist must remain very alert and aware that this is very damaging to the already severely damaged patient, as it repeats the pattern of abandonment and abuse.

When the therapist comes to the conclusion that he either cannot or is unwilling to do something for the patient, he must tell the patient in a personal manner and not hide behind the rules and regulations of the institute or practice where he works (see the section 'Empathic Confrontation'). The frustrations that are hereby elicited during therapy are simply a normal part of the therapeutic process, just as frustrations are a normal part of the childrearing process. The therapist can help the patient deal with these frustrations in an appropriate manner (see Chapter 9, 'Treatment Methods for the Angry/Impulsive Child').

Giving direction

Just as a parent gives advice and counsel to his children, the therapist also gives advice and opinions to encourage healthy development of the patient.

He also intervenes when he believes that the patient's behaviour could be damaging. This can take place when the patient engages in behaviours that interfere with therapy (e.g. missing many sessions) or when the patient refuses to talk about relevant topics during sessions. The therapist can make the patient aware of these behaviours and help to lay links between the behaviours and the schema modes that are responsible for them. Further, he can attempt to motivate the patient to change these behaviours. Damaging behaviours outside of therapy must also be addressed or one runs the risk of these behaviours interfering with any positive movement in the sessions. Examples of damaging behaviours are substance abuse, unhealthy or irregular eating, or continued involvement with friends/partners who are abusive. If the patient is involved in life-threatening behaviours or behaviours that threaten others, these must take priority. The therapist explains which mode leads to this behaviour and how the patient can stop it. If necessary he can help think of alternative behaviours. Should these actions not lead to an acceptable reduction in these behaviours, the therapist can refer back to limit setting (see 'Setting Limits'). Once the damaging behaviour is identified and stopped, the therapist should continue to ask the patient about this damaging behaviour (e.g. How is she doing? Is she still 'clean'?) until he is absolutely certain that the problem is no longer an issue.

When a patient has problems with her relationships, the therapist should first attempt to get an idea of the other person involved. He can ask, for example, that she brings her partner to a session. If the patient does not want to involve her partner in therapy or her partner does not want to participate in therapy, the therapist must respect this choice and rely on information obtained from the patient in order to get an idea of the partner and the situation. If the therapist thinks that the partner has a good influence on the patient, he can help them solve their relationship problems and use psycho-education about BPD. By educating the patient's partner about BPD, the therapist can help him better understand what is going on during difficult periods. Together they can discuss what to do to help prevent conflicts from escalating and how they can work together to solve crises. If necessary the partner can come regularly and participate in discussions about the dysfunctional schemas. However, sometimes it is clear that the partner does not have the patient's best interests at heart and is actually trying to hurt the patient. This is particularly evident when abuse and/or mistreatment is taking place. This results in the patient continuously re-experiencing the painful issues of her past and the therapist must help protect the patient and advise her to leave her partner.

Empathic confrontation

The therapeutic relationship is not only a safe haven for the patient but must also serve as a source of change. Once a safe, close relationship has been developed between therapist and patient, the therapist can begin to confront the patient with the consequences of her behaviour. When doing this it is important that the therapist addresses his own feelings that the patient evokes in him by her behaviour during the sessions or by her descriptions of her behaviour outside of therapy towards others. Firstly, he explores whether his reaction is based on the patient's behaviour or that his own dysfunctional schemas are the underlying cause for his reaction (see 'Therapists' Schemas and Self-Disclosure'). After making sure that his own dysfunctional schemas are not interfering with his reaction, he must confront the patient in a friendly, personal but very clear manner. He is careful that it is the *behaviour* that he rejects, without rejecting the patient as a *person*. He should not hide behind abstract rules or norms (e.g. regulations of the institution where he works or a professional code of ethics), but rather deliver this message in a very honest and personal manner.

Sample dialogue: empathic confrontation

T: Nora, I notice that you are asking me to support you in the way you behaved last week towards your son's teacher. But I get the feeling that you want to force me into supporting you and that you will not allow me to have an opinion that differs from yours. This is very annoying for me. It makes me not say what I'm really thinking, but at the same time I know that when I do that, I'm not helping you.

P: (angry) Oh great, so you think I dealt with the teacher wrong too? Now you also think I'm an idiot!

T: No, that's not what I'm trying to tell you. I meant that because of the manner in which you try to force me into agreeing with your point of view, I don't dare share my real opinions with you. This would create a distance between us if it continues and I don't want that to happen.

P: (after a short silence … sad) Maybe you don't want that, but I feel like you're walking out on me too!

T: Yes, I understand that and I think what is happening between us now is something which often happens when people don't agree with you. You become very defensive and feel rejected and before you know it, you're right in the middle of your punitive mode and you think that everyone who doesn't agree with you thinks you're an idiot and rejects you. I do understand your reaction though. In the past you were never allowed to have your own opinion and your mother would make you out to be a fool whenever you said anything. But you have to realize that you're in a different situation now. I don't think you are stupid or a fool. I think that sometimes you deal with things well and other times not so well and I want to be able to tell you this without feeling forced into agreeing with you in everything. So I would like to ask you not to isolate yourself and shut me out, but to try to discuss the matter with me in a calm and relaxed way.

After confrontation, the patient will often become emotional and possibly experience the confrontation as punishment. In the example mentioned, Nora initially feels angry and this is replaced by a feeling of sadness. The therapist should first pay attention to these expressed emotions. He should then explain why he confronted her with her behaviour. After she has been confronted in this manner, there should be an opportunity to analyse why this happens to her so often and how this behaviour is linked to underlying schemas. One can further analyse how and why these ideas were developed and can begin replacing them with more functional views and schemas. Nora eventually developed new beliefs, 'if someone disagrees with me, that means they disagree with my ideas, not with me as a person.' In this way her underlying schema of not trusting people could slowly be broken down and replaced with more functional schemas.

Role playing and role reversal

Another way of confronting a patient with the effects of her behaviour is by role playing with role reversal. This is particularly effective when an explanation of the effects of the patient's behaviour on the therapist alone is ineffective. The therapist proposes that they reverse roles and then actually stands up and physically changes chairs with the patient. The therapist can then, for example, role play the protector mode by saying that there is nothing to discuss and everything is just fine. The patient (now playing the role of therapist) must try to think of a way to convince the therapist (now playing the role of patient in the protector mode) to talk about his problems. Usually most patients are very good in the role of the therapist and realize what is taking place in the session and why the therapist is stuck (in this case, in the patient's protector mode).

Setting limits

It is imperative in good parenting that clear limits are set. In addition to general limits on abuse, violence and suicide, there are also personal limits. As these differ for each therapist, there are no set guidelines on personal limits. However, the therapist is not meant to set too many limits or to do this too quickly. Setting limits is generally necessary when there is behaviour involved that could severely hinder the therapy. Initially, the therapist is easy-going and flexible as a good therapeutic relationship has to be established. Once this has been accomplished, the therapist's approach changes gradually later on in therapy. However, topics that often result in limit setting are:

1. Too much out-of-session contact or too many cancellations/missed sessions.
2. Unrealistic expectations regarding the nature of contact. For example, the patient can expect the therapist to put an arm around her when she is clearly emotional; however, the therapist may have the feeling that he is overstepping his personal boundaries.
3. Impulsive or destructive behaviour such as threatening the therapist or threatening to destroy items in his office and/or engaging in self-destructive behaviours.
4. Abuse of medication or other substances.

For a detailed list of examples of transgressing behaviour, refer to Table 4.2.

With due observance of professional codes of ethics, the rules and regulations of the institute where the therapist works and the law, each therapist will have his own personal boundaries. For example, a female therapist may have fewer apprehensions about putting her arm around the shoulders of a female patient compared with a male therapist. However, even here, personal choices are very often different and deliberation with a peer supervision group is imperative. On the one hand, there is a group of therapists who set too few limits. The members of the peer supervision group must be careful that they do not offer too much extra attention to the patient or do so for too long of a period of time. On the other hand, there is a group of therapists who may be too distanced and uncaring due to their fear of setting limits. These therapists are often concerned that the patient will begin to ask for more and more and eventually overwhelm the therapist. Here, the inability to set limits results in a less-than-optimum therapeutic attitude.

It is not the purpose of a peer supervision group to force their norms and values on its members. What one therapist may experience as exceeding his personal boundaries may be quite normal to another therapist. It is important that the therapist does not undertake anything with a patient that he is incapable of providing, or that is damaging to the patient.

By far the single most important reason for setting limits is the safety of both patient and therapist. When the therapist sets too few limits the patient will, having experienced too many transgressions in her childhood, possibly continue her boundary exploration. This can be damaging to the patient, for example, when the therapist does not set limits on self-injury. On the other hand it can also be damaging to the therapist in both a physical and psychological sense. This might result in the therapist's motivation to move on with therapy being strongly reduced. In this way the patient is again abandoned and thus one of her traumas for which she sought help is repeated.

When the relationship between the therapist and patient becomes too close, the therapist may not dare to frustrate the patient enough. This results in her inability to build frustration tolerance. In a worst-case scenario, the relationship develops into a personal friendship and is no longer therapeutic.

If the therapist feels that his boundaries have been crossed, he must immediately make this clear to the patient in a personal, non-punitive manner. Usually the patient does not know that the therapist has problems with her behaviour. The patient has a similar level of understanding as a child who at her birth does not know what her parents will and will not allow. Once the therapist explains the situation to the patient, he must also give her the opportunity to change her behaviour. Usually this suffices to set the boundary.

Sample dialogue: setting limits

Nora often arrived 5 to 10 minutes late for her sessions inducing a rushed feeling in the therapist because there usually was more than enough to discuss in a session. He had started to allow the sessions to continue until they were finished, which resulted in his being late for the next appointment. He noticed that he began to become irritated and that the sessions did not flow as well as previously. He decided to discuss this with Nora the next time she was late.

T: Nora, I've noticed that recently you have been 5 to 10 minutes late for your sessions and this really bothers me because then I feel rushed.

P: Yeah, I was late today, but I hadn't noticed that it happens so often.

T: It is possible that you haven't noticed. Perhaps that is because I've allowed your sessions to go over time, but then I feel rushed because I have to watch out not to start my next appointment too late.

P: Yes, I can see how that is annoying. But I'm dependent on the bus. If it's on time, then I'm on time.

T: Apparently the bus is not always reliable and on time. I understand that you are usually unaware that you're late. I would like to ask you to be on time for your sessions. Then I will not feel pressured and can pay closer attention to you and what you say, rather than the clock.

P: I'll see if I can catch the earlier bus.

After setting limits the therapist discusses which modes the patient experiences as an effect of the limit setting. In the case of Nora, the punitive parent may respond with something like: "You've made another big mistake and deserve to be punished." Little Nora then becomes scared and Angry Nora would become angry, feeling she is again being treated unfairly. Finally, the protector would probably decide not to attend the next session at all. The therapist can then discuss one or more of the possible reactions per mode in an appropriate manner (see Chapter 9). He should also discuss which mode made the patient transgress. Should Nora continue arriving late for her sessions, despite her good intentions, it could be the protector

Table 4.1 Steps in limit setting.

1. Explain the rule; use personal motivation. *when patient repeats the transgression*
2. Repeat the rule; show your feelings a little, repeat personal motivation. *when patient repeats the transgression*
3. As above; announce consequence (don't execute yet!). *when patient repeats the transgression*
4. Execute sanction. *when patient repeats the transgression*
5. As above; announce stronger consequence. *when patient repeats the transgression*
6. Execute stronger consequence. *when patient repeats the transgression*
7. Announce temporary break in therapy so that patient can think it over. *when patient repeats the transgression*
8. Execute temporary break in therapy so that patient can consider whether she wants the present therapy with this limit. *when patient repeats the transgression*
9. Announce end of treatment. *when patient repeats the transgression*
10. Stop treatment and refer the patient.

Based on Young (personal communication) and Arntz (2004).

mode attempting to keep the sessions short in order to avoid dealing with subjects she finds too painful or difficult.

Unfortunately setting limits is not always straightforward. It is a good idea to have a plan of steps ready that can be followed when setting limits. This should include how you set the limits, how they will be tightened and what sanctions you will set.

In Table 4.1 such steps are described. The word 'consequence' may be associated with punishment. However, in this instance it is used to indicate a consequence, not a punishment. All consequences must be naturally connected to the transgression as well as being feasible.

It is important that setting limits is a process that builds up and offers the patient the opportunity to change her behaviour. Because of this, all necessary steps are fully described in Table 4.1, finally ending with the most severe consequence, which would be the termination of therapy. Consequences setting in limit setting must take place gradually with the constant opportunity for change. For instance, repeated tardiness should not immediately result in cancelling the session. This would be an example of a very serious sanction and would not allow the patient the opportunity to change her behaviour. Examples of appropriate steps and sanctions can be seen in Table 4.2.

Make sure not to follow through the sanction before the patient has first been given the opportunity to follow the limit set; but if necessary, administer the sanction. Just as a parent must follow through with sanctions in childrearing, so too must the therapist. As in childrearing, not doing so will result in more trangressing behaviour.

Should the consequences not be helpful, a break in therapy will give the patient time to think and eventually choose whether or not she wishes to continue with the therapy. Often the enacting of consequences is unnecessary as the patient will adjust her behaviour once she is made aware of it. It is seldom that things go so far that there must be a break in therapy or therapy must be stopped.

In practice, most therapists have a tendency to wait too long to set limits. A therapist who does not set limits in a timely fashion may end up guilty of emotional distancing from his patient, or may secretly blame the patient for his own dissatisfaction and react in an overly irritated manner. This can also result in the premature ending of therapy.

Therapists' Schemas and Self-Disclosure

This therapy requires a long-term therapeutic relationship with patients who not only have very strong emotions themselves, but also arouse strong emotions in those around them. Because of this, it is of the utmost importance that the therapist has good personal insight and is aware when the behaviours of others are activating his own dysfunctional schemas. It is conceivable that the therapist is not confronted with such issues when he addresses short-term symptom-focused therapy. But as it is the therapeutic relationship that is an important means of change in this therapy, self-knowledge is essential. We will not go deeper into this subject in this book. Knowledge of literature on the subject (e.g. Beck *et al.*, 2004; Burns and Auerbach, 1996; Young and Klosko, 1994), personal (learning) therapy and a supportive peer supervision group may be necessary to practise this therapy successfully.

Table 4.2 Possible consequences for violating limits.

Common limit violations	Possible appropriate actions
Missed sessions	*Reduce contact outside of sessions. *Limit the following session to discussing the situation of not attending sessions. Skip one week.
Arriving too late (tardiness)	*Do not compensate by allowing the session to go over time. *Shorten the session by the amount of time that the patient was late. *Limit the topic of the session to tardiness. *Reduce the session to 10-minute discussion on tardiness.
Too much (telephone) contact outside of sessions	*Limit availability out of sessions to a regular moment in the day. *Limit length of each (telephone) conversation to a few minutes. *Limit number of available moments to a set number of times per week.
Aggressive behaviour towards therapist	*Ask that this be limited. *Ask patient to express herself using different words. *Ask patient to leave the room and return when her aggression is reduced. *Therapist leaves the room for a period of time.
Substance abuse (drug and/or alcohol)	*Make agreements on reducing use to normal levels. *During the session, only allow discussions about reduction of substance use. *Shorten session to a 10-minute discussion about substance abuse and repeat agreements about normal levels of use. *Temporary referral to drug/alcohol rehabilitation; continue infrequent sessions. *Stop therapy.
Medicine abuse	*Agreements on reducing use to normal. *Limit access to prescription refills (e.g. once a week). *Pick up medication from caregiver daily.
Defiant or aversive appearance	*Ask patient to adjust her appearance in a less distractive manner (e.g. button her blouse). *Turn chair so that you cannot look at the patient as much. *Ask patient to go home, change clothes and return later.
Gifts	*Return gift. *Tell patient that you will throw the gift away the next time and return gift. *Throw away gift. *Ask patient to take gift home with her.

A number of the more common pitfalls encountered in dealing with schemas are listed as follows. The relevant schema and coping strategies are shown in parentheses after each problem (see Appendix I):

- Waiting too long to set limits and/or setting too few limits and/or spending too much time with the patient outside of sessions (seeking patient's approval and/or self-sacrifice).
- Thinking that you are not doing well enough (unrelenting standards/ overly self-critical, or failure).
- Not discussing missed sessions (schema avoidance by the therapist, such as abandonment or emotional deprivation. Perhaps the therapist is afraid that the patient will stop therapy altogether if he approaches this subject and he cannot allow her to abandon him).
- Muting strong emotions (vulnerability or emotional inhibition).
- Abusing the patient in order to counterbalance/neutralize/negate own personal shortcomings (emotional deprivation, dependence or entitlement).
- Too cold and stand-offish when the patient needs support and under-standing (emotional inhibition).
- Overly critical when the patient makes mistakes (negativity, unrelenting standards, punitiveness).

The last three points in particular would render a therapist unfit for the practice of this therapy. BPD patients were denied understanding and support during their childhood and therefore require a great deal of both support and understanding from their therapist. A therapist who is overly critical and/or abuses the patient, reinforces the punitive mode, and is not able to offer emotional support to the little child mode of the patient.

Should the therapist become aware that he has trouble maintaining a good/healthy therapeutic relationship with certain patients, he can make a function analysis of the therapeutic relationship (see Figure 4.1).

The therapist must try to find a balance between close contact, fulfilling the needs of the patient which is necessary for therapy, while at the same time maintaining the necessary distance from the client. Should too much distance between the two occur, sharing something personal is a good manner of improving contact. This should take place at an appropriate moment in therapy and should involve a topic that the therapist himself is 'finished with'. In this manner, the therapist's self-disclosure of how he

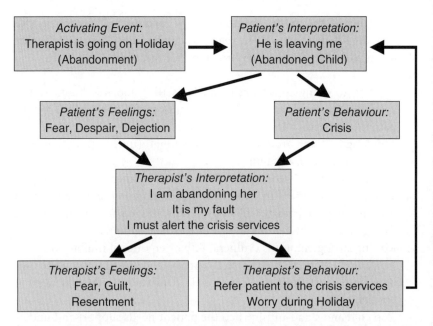

Figure 4.1 Example of functional analysis of the interaction between therapist and patient (from the therapist's perspective).

reacted to a difficult situation in his own life can be helpful in the therapeutic process. By doing so, the therapist carries out his role of setting an example for the patient by helping to put things into perspective and showing her that difficulties are not impossibilities.

Cognitive Techniques and the Therapeutic Relationship

If in a therapeutic relationship it becomes clear that the patient has certain dysfunctional cognitions regarding the therapist ('he thinks I'm a whiner') and the therapy ('I should have been finished with this therapy a long time ago') that are recurrent, one should discuss this using a cognitive approach when possible (see Chapter 6). The patient addresses these subjects by challenging her cognitions during the sessions or outside of the sessions. During the session the patient can check if her ideas about the therapist are correct. This requires the therapist to be as transparent as possible in his answers and not just explore why the patient has these thoughts about him (see Table 4.3).

Table 4.3   Cognitive diary on the therapeutic relationship.

Activating event	*Therapist yawns*
Feeling	Fear
Thoughts	He thinks I'm a whiner.
Behaviour	I don't say anything anymore.
Challenging my thoughts	What demonstrates that he thinks I'm so boring? He's yawning. Any more evidence? He just looked at his watch. What other explanations could there be for this? He always looks at his watch a couple of times during the sessions because he wants to make sure that there's enough time for me to talk about everything I want to discuss. But he never yawns. Maybe he's tired, after all it's almost his vacation time. What if he really thinks I'm boring, what would happen? I'm scared he will stop treating me. Does this make any sense at all given my previous experiences with him? No, when I ask him what he thinks, he tells me and he has never said that he thinks I'm boring or given any indication that he's considering ending therapy. He has said that sometimes I try too hard to tell everything in too much detail. Perhaps that's what I'm doing now. That means I'm not boring, but perhaps my story is boring.
What mode caused these thoughts?	The punishing mode causes me to think that it's my fault and that I'm boring. The protector mode results in me not wanting to talk anymore.
Desired reaction	*What would be a better way to look at this situation?* There's no way for me to know what he's thinking when he yawns. It's unnecessary to instantly conclude that his yawn is a result of me or my behaviour. *What would be a better way to solve this situation?* I could simply ask him what he thinks about me and if he thinks I'm boring.
Feeling	Relief

Behavioural Techniques and the Therapeutic Relationship

Behavioural techniques such as reinforcing desired behaviour (in particular therapy-enhancing behaviours) both within the therapy sessions as well as practising these behaviours outside of the sessions are an important part of ST.

Example of behavioural techniques and the therapeutic relationship

Nora had the tendency to look out of the window when she spoke of something that she was ashamed of. Because of this, she missed out on important information, in particular the non-verbal behaviour of the therapist. While she heard no rejection in his words, she thought she might see rejection in his face if she dared to look. He suggested that she should look at him more often and test if her theories were correct with the reality of what actually happened. After a while, she began to look at the therapist more often and sometimes even dared to share more of herself.

The therapist can also encourage the patient to try out certain behavioural experiments on him during the session.

Example of behavioural experimentation in the therapeutic relationship

Every now and then Nora would test her therapist by seeing if he would give a negative reaction when she said that she didn't understand something. She did this without telling her therapist. Only after she was confident that the dreaded rejection would not be a consequence, she told her therapist about her little experiment and was very surprised with the results. She wanted to know with certainty that the therapist did not think she was dumb.

The behaviour of the therapist during the entire therapeutic process is that of a role model for the patient, with the therapist modelling healthy behaviour for the patient. Assuming all goes well, he is an example of respectful, transparent, honest, interested, non-judgemental, trustworthy and balanced behaviour. The goal is for the patient to take on and adjust the different aspects of the therapist's behaviour in order to develop into a healthy adult.

Summary

Creating a safe therapeutic relationship is the central point of this therapy. While applying experiential, cognitive and behavioural techniques, the therapist continues to employ the described style of limited reparenting. Time and time again he will approach specific problems with a specific technique in a friendly but clear and determined manner, as this is also the best way to behave towards a child whom you want to teach something. He will balance the change of techniques so as not to overwhelm the patient on the one hand, and not under-stimulate her on the other. For example, when by using imagination strong emotions are triggered, it is sensible to take a little extra time during the next session to discuss what happened in the previous session and give it a place in a cognitive sense. `

In the following chapters we will discuss the different techniques: experiential techniques in Chapter 5, cognitive techniques in Chapter 6, behavioural techniques in Chapter 7, and specific methods and techniques in Chapter 8. This is followed by how one should apply these techniques to the different schema modes (Chapter 9).

5

Experiential Techniques

Therapeutic techniques that are directed at feelings (see Table 3.1) – also referred to as 'experiential techniques' – have an important role in treating BPD with ST. Most of these techniques can be used in current situations as well as with experiences from the patient's past. Because of this, the following paragraphs will address both present and past applications.

The following sections on imagery rescripting and historical role play are based on a paper by Arntz and Weertman (1999). Further references to this article are not given but should be assumed. This paper also discusses the theoretical background of these methods.

Imagery

During an imagery exercise the patient tries to recreate a certain situation in her mind. In doing so, she experiences as it were, what took place during interactions with others, and what her emotions are. Rescripting is later added when either patient or therapist feels that some aspects of the situation must be changed or altered.

Applications and aims of imagery

In the beginning of therapy, imagery can be used when one is looking for a connection between the patient's current schemas and events from

Schema Therapy for Borderline Personality Disorder. Arnoud Arntz and Hannie van Genderen
© 2009 John Wiley & Sons, Ltd.

the past. As therapy progresses and a safe therapeutic relationship has been established, imagery rescripting can be applied in the following situations:

- situations in which there was emotional, physical or sexual abuse (this includes traumatic situations with peers such as bullying);
- situations in which the patient's emotional, physical or developmental needs were not adequately met;
- curtailment of autonomy or expressing emotions;
- 'parentization' when the patient takes on the role of agent between parents (caregivers), or when the patient has to take care of (one of the) parents or brothers and sisters.

One of the most important goals of imagery rescripting is that the patient discovers that it is the situation in which she was raised that was 'wrong'; instead of thinking she is 'wrong'. Another important goal is the emotional processing of traumatic events. The schemas that the patient has developed based upon these inadequate situations are slowly replaced by healthier schemas. Note that imagery rescripting is different from imaginal exposure, which is a well-known treatment technique for PTSD. In imagery rescripting, exposure to the most traumatic moments is kept to a minimum, whereas actively changing the situation in imagery is the most important part.

Using imagery rescripting, the abandoned child can be protected and comforted, while the punishing side can be neutralized. The angry child can express her rage about the many violations of her rights and the healthy adult can learn when to take action when she sees situations in which the child was improperly treated.

Imagery rescripting helps the patient to become aware of her feelings and needs, and to learn better ways of dealing with them. She starts to ask for help and support from the people she trusts. Imagery rescripting sometimes leads to surprisingly quick change, but often requires to be repeatedly used with different situations and different memories in order to ensure lasting change.

In Figure 5.1 one can see that there are numerous starting and switching possibilities for imagery dependent upon what the therapy requires at that given moment.

Imagery can be started when the patient tells about a recent unpleasant situation. The therapist can then begin with her imagining a safe place and

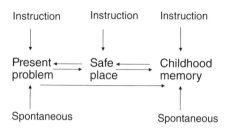

Figure 5.1 Pathways to childhood memories.

then follow with the unpleasant experience or he can start off directly with the unpleasant experience. This is followed by making a transition into the patient's past. The therapist can also suggest that they go directly back to an unpleasant situation from the patient's past if he is aware of such a situation in her past from the intake interview or other personal history from the patient. The main focus here is the type of (traumatic) experience that played a role in the formation of dysfunctional schemas.

Imagery of a safe place

It is a good idea to start introducing imagery by teaching the patient to imagine a safe situation. In this way, the patient can get used to imagery while at the same time creating a safe imaginary place she can return to at any given time should other imagery exercises become too intense and evoke unpleasant emotions. Ask the patient to close her eyes or if she finds this too uncomfortable, to pick a point on the floor and stare at it. Then ask her to imagine a safe place. This can be a real place where she has been to or knows of, or it can be a fantasy place. If the patient does not know of any safe places, the therapist can make suggestions, such as a place in nature or another place based on the intake interview where he thinks she is likely to feel safe. Some patients cannot think of a safe place because for them, the world is simply too dangerous and there are no safe havens. In such a situation, it is almost impossible for the patient to imagine a safe situation. For these patients it is of the utmost importance that the therapist allows a very strong, safe therapeutic relationship to develop. The therapist must actively protect the patient during imagery rescripting, so that safety is brought in by the therapist. The imagery of a safe situation is not a prerequisite to other forms of imagery exercises, so if the patient cannot imagine a safe place, the therapist should reassure the patient and proceed with finding a negative childhood memory.

During the subsequent discussion, a connection is made between the appearance of a mode in the here and now (punishing side) and a (traumatic) event in the patient's past.

A variation to this is to skip the unpleasant present situation and ask the patient to try and find a memory of her childhood directly. An example of

---

Using imagery in search for the roots of modes

In the first phase of the therapy, the search for the roots of modes is done using imagery without rescripting. For example, one can start off with imagining a safe place. Then the therapist can ask the patient to let this image go out of her mind and imagine an unpleasant situation that she currently experiences. It is also possible to start directly with the unpleasant situation. The patient is asked to pay particular attention to the unpleasant feelings this situation evokes and then to let this image go from her mind, but hold on to the feelings associated with the situation. The therapist continues by asking whether the patient has experienced this feeling as a child, and instructs the patient to hold the feeling and wait until a specific memory pops up. The patient should not look for a specific memory in a controlled way, but rather wait for a spontaneous association. The patient is then asked to describe the childhood situation in as much detail as possible. Once the image is clear she may return to her safe place and open her eyes again. It is of particular importance that the patient experiences this situation as if it is happening (again) in reality. The therapist asks her to use the present tense and imagine as many details about the situation as possible. By asking direct questions the therapist can help to clarify the situation and thereby assist the patient in this process (see phase 1, Table 5.1).

Sample dialogue of searching for the roots of modes

T: Close your eyes and imagine a safe place in the here and now.
P: I see myself sitting on the sofa with the cat on my lap.
T: You're sitting on the sofa with the cat on your lap and how do you feel?
P: Lovely, relaxed. I don't have to do anything.
T: OK, concentrate on that feeling.

(short silence)

T: Let go of that relaxed feeling and let rise a situation in the here and now which is unpleasant for you.

P: I forgot to give an important letter to my boss. He looked really angry.

T: How do you feel?

P: I'm scared.

T: What happens now?

P: I say that there were a lot of phone calls and I was very busy. But he just brushes me aside and starts reading the letter.

T: And how do you feel now?

P: Stupid, inferior, bad.

T: Hold on to that feeling, but let go of the image and see whether a memory of a situation from your childhood which gave you that same feeling pops up.

P: I don't know.

T: Try to hold on to that feeling of being stupid and inferior. You don't have to actively look for situations, they will come in time. But hold on to that feeling.

P: Now I can remember a situation at school. I didn't understand what the teacher was explaining and she made me look like a fool in front of the entire class.

T: You're at school. How old are you? Where are you physically in the class?

P: I am in the third grade. I'm standing at the board and I write the wrong thing on the board.

T: What happens now?

P: The teacher walks towards me and crosses out the word and says in a nasty, angry voice "Nora, you nitwit , sit down, you can't do this." And all of the children are laughing at me.

T: How do you feel now?

P: I'm so embarrassed! I wish the ground would just swallow me up. I want to cry, but I don't.

T: So you feel very sad and you're embarrassed because the teacher is so angry.

(patient nods)

T: I think that's clear and enough for right now. You can let go of this situation and that feeling and return to your safe place. On the sofa with the cat.

(The therapist leads the patient back to the safe place and then asks her to open her eyes.)

Table 5.1   Questions during imagery rescripting.

Phase 1	What is happening?
	What do you see? (hear, smell (other senses)?)
	Who is there with you?
	How old are you?
	What do you feel?
	What do you need?
Phase 2 (in three-phase model)	The above, plus:
	What do you think about this?
	What do you want to do?
	OK, do it.
Phase 3 (in three-phase model) (or phase 2 in two-phase model)	Partially the same as above, plus:
	What do you need?
	OK, ask X (X is the healthy adult (therapist, helper, adult self))
	(Allow Little Nora to ask the healthy adult; in this way the exercise also becomes an exercise in expressing her needs.)
	What is happening?
	What do you feel?
	Is that good?
	Is there something else you need? (continue until OK)
Repeat or change parts until the patient agrees that it is good.	

this method is asking the patient to 'picture Little Nora together with her mother. Look at mother. What happens? How do you feel?'.

Imagery Rescripting

In a later phase of therapy, imagery exercises are expanded to include rescripting. While the immediate reasons for using this method might be very diverse, the central goal remains the same, that is, that of changing the meaning attached to the past experiences. The therapist explains that while it is not possible to change the past, it is possible to change the conclusions one makes based upon the past.

For BPD patients, rescripting initially takes place in two main phases. In the first phase, the patient imagines the (traumatic) childhood memory from the perspective of the little child, in the second phase the therapist enters the image to rescript. In later phases of treatment, the patient may start to rescript herself by entering the image as a healthy adult. Then a third rescripting phase is added in which the patient experiences her adult rescripting from the perspective of the little child and asks for additional actions from the adult if she needs them. For obvious reasons this can only take place once the patient has developed a strong and healthy adult mode. The basic two-phase model for imagery rescripting is described in the following section. The three-phase model follows in the next section.

Basic model for imagery rescripting during the first part of the therapy

During the first part of treatment the patient has not yet achieved a strong enough healthy adult mode. Because of this she does not understand normal parent–child relationships and is not capable of imagining how a parent would (or should) react to a given situation. This inability to understand a normal parent–child relationship can be very serious and far-reaching. Some patients have no knowledge of basic life skills or the ability to care for themselves. As a child, they lived a rough life on the streets, or did their best to make themselves invisible at home, where they had to take care of themselves. It is easy to understand how such an individual would have no idea of how a 'normal parent' would react to a child who did something wrong, or if something terrible happened to the child. The therapist must therefore represent a model of good parenthood (see Chapter 4, 'Limited Reparenting'). In imagery rescripting exercises the therapist has to think how a healthy parent would react in the given situation. It is not necessary for the therapist to actually have children of his own in order for him to be aware of the appropriate parental response to a given situation. Usually, common sense and sound feelings will do. We will now describe how this two-phase imagery rescripting takes place. Table 5.2 presents an overview.

Phase 1: Imagining the original situation

The precursor to phase 1 involves the patient imagining a safe place or a recent unpleasant situation. The therapist can make use of information

Table 5.2   The two phases of the basic model of imagery rescripting during the first phase of therapy.

Phase 1	Patient = child	Original situation as the patient experienced it
Phase 2	Patient = child Therapist rescripts	Rescripting: the therapist rescripts the situation. The patient experiences the intervention of the therapist as a child. She requests and receives as much intervention from the therapist as she deems necessary.

from the patient's background as a starting point for the imagery (see Figure 5.1).

The patient imagines an unpleasant situation from her childhood in as much detail as possible. This does not have to be the most traumatic event she has experienced, as less powerful events also resulted in faulty conclusions and contributed to dysfunctional schemas. It is also unnecessary for the patient to recall her earliest memory as the events related to the formation of dysfunctional modes usually repeatedly took place, and a memory that is triggered is usually exemplary. Further, it is not important to be completely sure whether all the details are 100% accurately remembered or not. The purpose of this exercise is not to search for the absolute factual truth, but rather to change the meaning of the generalized schematic representations of typical experiences from the patient's childhood.

While the patient attempts to recall a concrete situation and to experience it from the perspective of the little child, the therapist continues to ask about her feelings and experiences. The therapist inquires as to sensory experiences (What do you see, hear, smell, feel?), to emotions (What do you feel? Are you angry or frightened?), to thoughts (What are you thinking now?) and to behaviours (What are you doing? What is happening?) (also see Table 5.1). Strong emotions are usually a good indicator that one is dealing with an important memory.

Example of phase 1 imagery

Nora is eight years old and has had a bad fall from her bicycle and cut her leg on barbed wire. Her mother does not help or comfort her. She is angry with Nora and spanks her.

P: I'm in the kitchen with my mother.

T: What happens there?

P: I fell and my leg is really bleeding. I'm crying.

T: How do you feel?

P: It hurts and I'm scared because it's a pretty deep cut from barbed wire.

T: What do you do?

P: I ask my mother to help me, but she yells at me to stop whining. She says my leg will get better on its own. She wants to know if the bike is damaged. ...

T: and then?

P: I'm afraid to say anything because the bike's wheel is bent out of shape. My mother turns to spank me. (Patient begins to cry and shake.)

T: OK, let's stop. We have enough and don't need to relive the entire situation.

Once the memory is clear, one may proceed to phase 2. It is unnecessary to relive the entire memory. It is enough that the patient experiences the emotions attached to the situation/memory. Sometimes it is helpful to discuss phase 1, but generally the therapist can suggest that the patient closes her eyes and phase 2 may begin.

Phase 2: Rescripting by the therapist

At the moment when something serious threatens to take place in the imagery, the therapist stops the situation and says that he is there to help Little Nora. He asks the patient to imagine that he is in the same place with her at that moment.

Example of phase 2: The therapist appears in imagery

T: I'm coming into the kitchen. Can you see me?

(patient nods)

T: I'm standing between you and your mother. I'm stopping her from raising her arm to hit you. Do you see that?

P: Yes, but be careful, she's very strong.

This is followed by the therapist doing anything and everything necessary to protect and comfort Little Nora. He stops the attacker and, if necessary, sends him/her away. If necessary, the therapist can use fantasy to protect the child from being attacked. He can suddenly become much stronger or larger in order to stop a violent attacker. He may also enlist the help of the police or child protective services.

Example of phase 2: The therapist appears in imagery and intervenes (continued)

T: I say to your mother "STOP, you may not hit Nora. Don't you see that she's seriously injured?!?"

P: Watch out, my mother is bigger than you are.

T: Don't worry, I may be small, but I'm very strong. I'm holding your mother's arm. What happens now?

P: My mother is very angry with you. I see it in her face, but she doesn't dare hit me as long as you're here.

T: Mrs. X your daughter needs to see a doctor; that looks like a very nasty cut.

P: Now my mother is swearing at you and says that I'm a pain in the ass and. …

T: Stop that immediately and leave Nora alone. She needs medical treatment.

P: She wants to hit you.

T: I'm picking her up and putting her in the hallway, out of the kitchen and I lock the door. She's gone!

P: Yeah now she can't hit you.

T: And she can't hit you either. She may not come back in as long as she behaves like that.

Once the attacker has been sent away, the imagery continues. Little Nora also needs support, comfort and care. She is usually very shocked and worried about what will happen next. Just as a good parent cares for his child, the therapist must also continue to care for the patient once the threat of attack is gone. He can do everything a 'real' parent would do to reassure a child such as speaking in a reassuring tone or manner and comforting the patient by sitting next to her or having her sit on his lap. The patient experiences this moment as a young child and she will find this very normal and feel very supported and reassured by this act. The patient also finds it supportive when the therapist follows such an unpleasant situation with a very pleasant situation such as playing a game, going for a walk or having ice cream.

Example of phase 2: The therapist helps and comforts during imagery

T: How are you doing Nora?

P: I'm still scared because soon she'll come back in and hit me. And now she's even madder because you helped me.

T: Then I think it's a good idea if she's locked up somewhere where she cannot get you. Where shall I lock her up? In jail?

P: Yes, but far away and somewhere where she can't escape.

T: OK I'll have her locked up on an island on the other side of the world. How do you feel now?

P: Calmer but still very sad.

T: You're still very sad. I see that as well. What do you need?

P: I don't know. I feel so alone now! (crying)

T: Shall I come and sit next to you? Would you like a tissue? Let me put my arm around you. It's OK, she's gone and I'm going to help take care of your leg. I'll call the doctor and say that he needs to come here and take a look at it.

(patient sighs and slowly begins to stop crying)

T: How do you feel now?

P: Much better. Is the doctor really going to come here for me?

T: Of course, because your leg looks very bad and I don't think you can walk to the doctor's office.

P: OK he can come in, but please stay with me because it really hurts.

(patient remains agitated and looks anxious)

Often the patient is also frightened of the later consequences that this care and attention will have in the long term and she must be reassured about the future. The child fears punishment for expressing her needs or being helped by the therapist. The therapist must make sure that the child understands how to contact the therapist if something goes wrong. Because this all takes place within the framework of imagery, it is possible to use both realistic (a cellphone) or fantasy (a magic spell) methods of reassurance. The situation can appear so unsafe for the patient that it is not sufficient for the therapist to return when the patient needs him. In this case, the therapist can suggest that he takes the patient to look for a safe place to live, for example with a nice family she knows, or with the therapist. The essential point of this intervention is that the patient feels safe and experiences the therapist as supportive.

Example of phase 2: The therapist takes the patient to a safe place during imagery

T: Is there something else you want to say?

P: Yeah, I'm scared that my mother will come back and really let me have it because I said you should lock her up.

T: So you're scared of being left here alone?

(patient nods)

T: Is there anybody who you could live with? Anybody who is nice to you and who would like to take care of you?

P: Perhaps Auntie Rose ... Yes, she is always nice to me.

T: Shall I take you to your Auntie's? You'll be safe there and you can call me if you need to.

(at last the patient begins to relax and carefully laugh)

T: Come with me, does your Auntie live far away?

(patient shakes her head no)

T: I take you to her house. ... So, here we are. Let's ring the bell. Your Auntie opens the door and is very happy to see you. Do you see that?

(patient nods and smiles)

T: Auntie Rose, I've brought Nora to you because she's had a nasty fall from her bike and I have called the doctor to come to check out her leg and she would like to stay here with you.

T: (to patient) What does your Auntie say?

P: She says it is fine and has me sit on the sofa by the TV.

T: OK we'll wait for the doctor and then I'll leave. I'll arrange it with your Auntie that you can live with her, and that I visit you daily until you're better. What do you think of that?

P: That's nice.

T: Is that enough or are there other things you would like?

P: No, this is good. I'm glad that I can stay with Aunt Rose and that you'll visit me every day.

After this, the patient may stop the exercise and discuss the meaning of this imagery in terms of her schemas. Returning to a safe place is unnecessary in this case as the patient has been brought to a safe place in the therapist's rescripting of the situation. In many cases the patient had already concluded that everything was her fault and that her parent had the right to be angry with her or mistreat her because she was a dumb, bad or lazy child. By rescripting the situation the patient becomes aware that she was not wrong and that she did not deserve the mistreatment, but rather that she was a small child who was in need of care and that her parent did things that a normal parent simply would not do. Her self-image, which still tells her that she is bad, dumb or lazy when she makes mistakes, can be adjusted using this technique. Whenever possible an alternative interpretation can be formulated and written out so that the patient can take this home with her. In any case, the most important issue is that the patient starts to feel about herself in a healthier way. "I wasn't guilty of the situation, but rather my mother should have kept her hands to herself and. ... I feel relaxed and not nearly as scared."

Imagery Rescripting in the Second Part of Treatment

Once a patient has moved along further in the therapeutic process and has developed her healthy adult mode, she herself can execute the rescripting. Now imagery rescripting has three phases (see Table 5.3). The first phase is identical to the first phase previously mentioned. Phases 2 and 3, while slightly different from phase 2 described earlier, retain the same essential points of protecting and comforting the child while helping her to adjust her faulty conclusions.

Table 5.3   The three phases of the basic model for imagery rescripting during the second phase of therapy.

Phase 1	Patient = child	Original situation as experienced by patient
Phase 2	Patient = adult	Rescripting: situation evaluated by patient as an adult. Patient intervenes as an adult
Phase 3	Patient = child	Rescripting: patient experiences the intervention of the adult as a child. She requests and receives additional interventions from the adult.

Phase 2: Rescripting by the patient as a healthy adult

After phase 1, the patient is asked to imagine entering the situation as a healthy adult. The therapist continues to ask the patient about her feelings and thoughts and what, from her healthy adult perspective, she thinks should be done for the little child. It is not the purpose of the therapist to impose opinions or actions on the patient. It is far more effective for her self-confidence when she makes these decisions for herself.

Sample of imagery with Big Nora as a healthy adult rescripting

T: You're now Big Nora. Can you imagine that?

P: Yeah a bit.

T: You are in the kitchen and you see what is happening to Little Nora.

P: I see her mother is very angry and wants to hit her.

T: What do you want to do?

P: I want to stop her and tell her that she needs to take care of Little Nora's injuries.

T: OK, do that.

P: Leave her alone and get her some help.

T: What is your mother doing now?

P: She's even madder, but I'm stronger and I take her out of the room.

T: Good job! How is Little Nora now?

P: OK, she is relieved and glad she didn't get hit.

Take note that the patient, when she intervenes as a healthy adult, not only takes action against the people who maltreat the child, but also pays attention to the little child. The therapist can ask the patient, while in the role of a healthy adult, if she knows/sees anything else the little child may need. If so, the therapist stimulates the healthy adult to do what she thinks should be done. If the patient thinks that everything is OK and the child's needs have been met, she can move to phase 3 and actually check to see if the child's needs have been met.

Variations with a patient only partially capable of being in the healthy adult mode

When the patient is in a healthy adult mode, but is unsure of how to continue further, there are two variations of phase 2 that can be used: either a helper is sought, or the therapist coaches the patient.

A helper can be someone from the patient's past (e.g. a relative or teacher), from her current situation (e.g. a partner or friend) or a fantasy figure (e.g. Superman). The therapist asks the patient to think of someone who could help support her to become and behave as a healthy adult and act against the aggressor or abusing adult; someone who can help protect the child. The therapist agrees with any helper who appears to have a healthy, positive influence, but will refuse those whom he knows as being negative or abusive either currently or in the patient's past. The patient is asked to have the helper join her in the imagery exercise and that he/she does or says things the patient is unable or afraid to do or say. The advantage of intervention by a helper instead of the therapist is that the patient herself must decide what the helper says and does and in this way becomes more actively aware of what an appropriate response should be as well as more aware of what a child's needs truly are. The patient's share is greater and her own feelings of self-worth and value are strengthened.

If the patient is unable to think of an appropriate helper, the therapist can try to coach her by suggesting things to say or behaviour that is related to what she had earlier thought of. This is particularly helpful the first time the patient tries to rescript from the healthy adult perspective, and also when she says appropriate things but does not fully succeed in stopping abuse or sending away a punitive parent. In any case, it is important that the maltreatment is stopped in phase 2, otherwise the little child cannot feel safe, and feeling safe is one of the ultimate goals of imagery rescripting.

Phase 3: Rescripting experienced by the child

The aim of phase 3 is to check if the little child has received the support she requires in order to meet her needs and to better integrate this new experience into her (childish) schema. The therapist asks the patient to close her eyes again and return to the little child in the imagery situation, viewing the intervention by the patient as an adult. The therapist describes what Big Nora does and asks the little child how she feels and thinks about the intervention Big Nora has made. Are there other things she needs or wishes to change? The therapist then prompts Little Nora to ask Big Nora for it, and to imagine what happens next.

The therapist continues to ask these questions until all of Little Nora's needs have been met. In this manner the patient can integrate new insights in her self-image. In the third phase the patient extends the rescripting in such a way that not only the threat is eliminated, but that also her other needs are met. In this way she learns to acknowledge her needs and to express her needs to others.

Example of imagery rescripting, phase 3: The little child is asked if she has further needs

T: You're now Little Nora again and in the kitchen with your mother.

(patient nods)

T: You see Big Nora coming in and just at the moment your mother is going to hit you, she stops her. She says that your mother cannot hit you and must take care of your injured leg. What do you think of that?
P: Good, now she can't hit me. But my mother is still angry.
T: Certainly! And now Big Nora puts her outside. How do you feel now?
P: Better.
T: Is it better or is there something else you need?
P: My leg still hurts and I'm very shaken up by the whole thing.
T: Tell that to Big Nora.
P: I'm still bleeding and my leg hurts and I'm scared.
T: Big Nora can see that and is getting the doctor and then she's sitting next to you. Is that better?

(patient nods and appears relieved)

T: How do you feel now? Is everything OK?
P: I need a hug and a tissue.
T: OK, ask her!
P: Can you give me a tissue and hug me?
T: What is Big Nora doing?
P: She gives me a tissue and hugs me.
T: How does that feel? (after some time) Is there anything else that you need? Is there anything else you want Big Nora to do?

If necessary, Big Nora can take her to Aunt Rose's house as in the example of phase 2 rescripting. However, it is also possible that the patient asks Big Nora to stay and care for her and that this is more appropriate to this phase of treatment.

After this third phase, as with the second phase, patient and therapist reflect on the implication of the rescripting and the emerged needs, feelings, and new insights for the adjustment of dysfunctional schemas.

Imagery Rescripting: Changing Behaviour Patterns

Imagery is a very helpful tool in changing behaviour patterns. Trying out new behaviours is often hindered by the patient's dysfunctional approach to dealing with problems.

The patient herself often does not know why attempting these new behaviours is problematic for her. Imagining a recent situation in which she did not succeed in trying out new behaviour, allowing the patient to describe the entire situation in detail, is sometimes more helpful as a form of information gathering than simply asking for a verbal description of the situation. Rescripting is then directed towards what the patient would like to have seen happen, but was unable to achieve. During the imagery she can practise effective ways of problem solving.

Young, Klosko and Weishaar (2003) describe imagery in which the patient describes the block and attempts to work through it: "For example, the block might look like a dark weight pressing down on the patient. On questioning, the patient reveals that the block conveys the same message as a pessimistic parent. The patient pushes the message away by pushing away the block."

Example of imagery rescripting: Changing behaviour patterns

For a long time, Nora has been unsure of what she wants to do with her life. She does not know if she wants to study or work. She is completely unclear as to in which direction she may even wish to develop. The therapist suggests that it might be a good idea to try and investigate this blockage in an imagery exercise.

T: Close your eyes and imagine that you're in a quiet, peaceful place. Where are you?

P: I'm walking in the park with Rob.

T: You're walking with Rob and he asks you what you're going to do with the rest of your life.

P: My first reaction is to change the subject.

T: It's good that you're aware of this. Try to think of another reaction to his question.

P: I tell him I don't know and need to think about it.

T: OK start thinking about it.

P: I can't, I feel paralysed.

T: What do you mean 'paralysed'? What or who is paralysing you?

P: The thought that I must make the right decision and can't try something out first. It feels like I'm tied to whatever decision I make.

T: Try to loosen those ties. Of course you can try different possibilities out and make mistakes. This idea that you cannot make mistakes comes from your father, but he is no longer allowed to hold you back.

P: Yes, that is right, but making decisions is still frightening for me … the possibility of making mistakes.

T: Try to free yourself from these ideas and begin to think of different possibilities.

P: OK that feels a bit strange, but not as paralysing.

T: So what's holding you back from thinking about your future is your fear of making mistakes and that's why you continue to avoid the subject.

The therapist can now ask the patient while she is in the process of imagery to think about what she wants to do in the future and share these thoughts with Rob. Another possibility is to stop the imagery exercise and discuss how she can learn to acknowledge this blockage at an early stage and teach her how to break through her tendencies of avoidance.

Other situations that the patient may be avoiding, despite having achieved the level of a healthy adult, may also be dealt with using imagery. This is particularly helpful when the patient is embarking on a new relationship and her old schemas and modes are becoming active again. The patient can try out new behaviours in imagery and test out which styles and approaches best fit her.

Problems with Using Imagery Rescripting

The use of imagery rescripting can be hindered by various different problems. The most common and significant problems faced during this therapeutic exercise are the following:

The patient does not close her eyes – With her eyes closed she can concentrate better on the exercise; however, this can also be achieved by staring at a fixed point or focal point in the room. Sometimes the patient cannot close her eyes or does not dare to do so because of the fear of being looked at or judged by the therapist. She may also fear that the therapist may do something unexpected. First, the reasons for not daring to close the eyes are explored. Then the patient can make suggestions to the therapist which would help her to feel safer; for example, that the therapist also closes his eyes or turns his chair or physically moves away from the patient. The therapist can also suggest that the patient tries closing her eyes for one or two minutes to get an idea of what it will feel like, and then propose a gradual increase in the length of time having her eyes closed.

Which memories should you choose? – It can be very threatening when the patient is flooded with many memories that often overlap one another. If she is unable to choose one memory, this can be a sign that her life is still too chaotic and she must first organize herself before starting imagery exercises. If the patient can choose a memory, try to choose one during which the patient was young. When she is young it is self-evident that the child cannot be expected to act like an adult or to take adult responsibilities like running the house or taking care of a baby. Further, at this young age it is easier quickly and clearly to make the patient aware that overly punitive punishment and/or (sexual) abuse was the responsibility of the parent(s) and not the child.

Continual repetition of the same memory – When the patient continually brings up the same memory and the therapist knows that important experiences from her past have not been addressed, there is perhaps avoidance of painful subjects. The therapist can suggest dealing with these subjects by means of imagery and explain that it is important to rework these events with rescripting as well because they are important influences of her dysfunctional schemas.

Inability to 'find' memories – If the patient says she has no memories from her youth, it is likely that she consciously does not want to be reminded of these memories or that she has buried them away and actually does have difficulty remembering them. By using imagery to recall a pleasant memory, often memories of very unpleasant situations can emerge. Should the fear of painful memories or punishment play a large role for the patient, it is helpful to acknowledge these feelings and explore which modes are involved. The punitive parent mode in particular should be addressed immediately. After effectively dealing with interfering modes, imagery work is often possible. When there is a high fear of losing control, the therapist must allow the patient as much control as possible in the imagery. The therapist can first ask the patient to try – with her eyes open – to look at a focal point or agree upon a certain length of time. This gives her more control and a greater feeling of safety. Should this prove to be too threatening, then it is likely that it is too early in the therapeutic process for this technique and the therapist must work further on developing a trusting relationship. If the patient disassociates, the therapist must stop the exercise and bring the patient out of this state. Possibly, more security in the therapeutic relationship must be established before imagery can be attempted again. In many cases, simply continually attempting to do imagery will lead to a childhood memory.

The patient does not want anybody to go against her parent(s) – What do you do when a patient refuses or is unable to act against a punitive parent out of a misplaced sense of loyalty? One can explain that the purpose is not to reject her parent(s) completely as they are now, but rather to address the *behaviours* her parent(s) expressed during her youth that are related to the formation of her dysfunctional schemas. She need not reject everything about her parent(s), but she must weigh which values and norms she wishes to retain from her parents and which she wishes to reject.

The patient thinks the intervention is wrong – Every now and then, after the rescripting, the patient may be dissatisfied with her own intervention or that of the therapist. In that case, phase 2 can be repeated using a different intervention. If, for example, the patient first wants to have Big Nora or a helper beat up her mother as a form of revenge, but on second thoughts decides locking her away in a prison is a better idea, then this is changed in the imagery. However, with each rescripting it remains necessary to protect and help the little child. An imagery exercise that allows an abusive or violent parent to continue abusing results in the trauma being repeated. Should this situation arise, the therapist must immediately intervene and stop the abusive parent.

The patient finds the intervention unrealistic – The simplest solution to this problem is to think up a different intervention. However, sometimes this does not work and the patient's fear of becoming overly emotional plays too large a role. The protector attempts to escape by declaring that the intervention is unrealistic. If this is the case, the therapist must support the patient as much as possible so that she tries. In other cases, the therapist can explain that, despite imagery rescripting being a fantasy technique, it is extremely helpful in processing memories of childhood experiences that underlie her present problems. Some patients like some explanation about the plasticity of memory, while others feel reassured by explaining the empirical evidence for the technique.

Guilt feelings – If the patient feels guilty because she did not do anything to stop the abuse when she was a child, it is reassuring to explain to the patient exactly what children of that particular age are normally capable of doing. Remember, her knowledge of normal development is often severely limited. By observing children in her direct environment, the patient can be made aware of just how small and young a child of, say, four years old actually is and how little control she has over her life and surroundings. The therapist can also use examples from his own childhood as samples of a 'normal' childhood.

The patient only reports later childhood memories – Some patients report memories of their later childhood, say after 13 years, but cannot find earlier memories. The therapist can ask the patient to try to find, via the adolescent memory, earlier childhood memories. Another possibility is to ask the patient to remember an early childhood situation known from the amanuensis or other sources. Often however, a specific mode interferes with this; for example, the detached protector (preventing strong emotions and helplessness) or the punishing parent mode (a rebellious adolescent is easy to blame). In such cases, techniques appropriate for these modes should be used first (see Chapter 9).

The patient is unable to put herself in the child's perspective – This is a common problem for patients who were forced into semi-parenthood as children. They were required, out of necessity, to behave as 'adults' at a young age and have a very limited concept of how a child experiences the world. The therapist must attempt to take over the parental responsibilities from the little child and pass them on to a responsible other (e.g. child welfare services, a social worker, another therapist). Only then can the patient feel free enough to experience her own needs. Another method to help the patient feel more like a child is for the therapist to talk to her during imagery in the way an adult speaks to a child.

Imagery rescripting is a powerful tool to evoke changes in the patient's schemas. As previously mentioned, with BPD patients, this technique is not continuously used in numerous, consecutive sessions. However, therapist and patient may both avoid imagery rescripting and therefore it is wise to plan the use of it during a prolonged period once every two sessions. Alteration of imagery rescripting with other experiential as well as cognitive and behavioural techniques is recommended.

Role Play

Role play directed at changing schemas can be helpful in dealing with situations from the patient's past as well as from recent events. Role play focused on the patient's childhood, also referred to as 'historical role play', can result in strong results, similar to those seen in imagery rescripting. It depends on the therapist's and patient's preferences as to which method is most often used.

The areas of application for the use of historical role play are similar to those of imagery rescripting (see the beginning of this chapter). For obvious reasons, the therapist cannot play the role of an abusive parent. Abuse is therefore most often dealt with by imagery rescripting.

Another difference between imagery rescripting and role play is that the latter can also be used to give the patient more insight into her own part in the interactions with her parent(s) as well as to the motivation that her parent(s) could have had, which the patient did not experience as a child (see 'Phase 2: Role Switching').

The absence of the father during childhood may be experienced by the patient as rejection and a lack of love. This contributed to her feelings of inferiority. When doing role play, it becomes evident that her father did in fact love his daughter, but stayed away to avoid arguments with the mother. The absence of attention is correct; however, the patient's conclusion that this was based on her father finding her an unworthy daughter was found to be a faulty assumption.

This form of role playing is indicated for clarifying ambiguous situations. That is, situations in which the parent's behaviour was indeed dysfunctional, but not motivated by rejection of her as a little child.

Historical role play

In preparing for role play, both patient and therapist search for relevant experiences from the patient's past. Often there are a number of current situations in which the patient is regularly stuck. These are usually linked to events from her past, which are similar to these current situations. In Nora's situation, she continually got stuck in situations at her work when she felt others ignored her feelings. She would then become frightened and wait around feeling isolated. She thought that her superiors did not see that others were ignoring her and felt they would label her a complainer if she herself brought this to their attention. When a relevant situation in her past is found, therapist and patient explore which schemas or modes were developed or strengthened by it. This is followed by a three-phase role play (see Table 5.4).

It is important that different chairs are used during role play from the regular chairs and/or places used by the patient and therapist during 'normal' sessions. This helps to avoid role confusion. Just as with other forms of role playing, the situation is enhanced by the furniture and items in the therapist's office. The patient must immerse herself in the past

Table 5.4 The three phases of historical role playing.

	Division of roles	*Role play*
Phase 1	Patient = child Therapist = the other person	Original situation
Phase 2	Patient = the other person Therapist = the child	Original situation; role switching The patient experiences the perspective of the other person involved in the situation.
Phase 3	Patient = child Therapist = the other person	Patient now tries out this new behaviour.

situation as much as possible. She must try to become the actual eight-year-old Nora as much as possible in order to relive the feelings and be able to draw the same conclusions. To help this process, both patient and therapist use the present tense when speaking. The therapist does his best to accurately imitate the parent or other individuals involved.

If more individuals aside from therapist and patient are required in order to allow a more accurate role play (e.g. due to gender differences), one can ask others to be involved in the role play (e.g. friends of the patient or colleagues of the therapist).

Phase 1: The original situation

The original situation is acted out. The patient plays the role of the child and the therapist plays the role of the other significant person (usually the parent) as directed by the patient. Role play must involve a concrete moment in which the patient developed dysfunctional ideas in her past. The role play should not take very long. The patient describes the situation as accurately as possible, as well as providing information as to the behaviour of the person the therapist is playing. The therapist must ask as much about the individual he is playing in order to accurately 'become' that person. This preparation should not take half of the session, but should be brief. If not, there is a strong chance that all three phases of the role play will not be completed during a single session. Whether or not the role play is in fact accurate will be evident during the role play itself.

Sample of historical role play phase 1: Enacting the situation

Situation: Nora is depressed because her colleagues have not involved her in the yearly personnel's outing. This reminds her of when she was bullied at school and no one helped her. The concrete situation is that she comes home from school and tells her mother that she is being bullied at school. Her mother (M) does not react.

Role Play 1: Enacting the situation

The therapist plays the mother. He is standing by the table and is busy cleaning. The patient is Nora, eight years old, and has just come home from school.

P: Mum, they are bullying me at school again. They took my new pen
          and broke it.
T = M: (annoyed) I'm busy; I don't have time for this.
P: But now it's broken and doesn't. ...
T = M: Not now! I already told you!

(patient walks away with a sigh)

After the first phase, patient and therapist return to their own chairs and discuss whether or not the role play was accurate in terms of the actual situation and whether or not the same emotions were evoked. If the role play was not accurate, then the patient must provide extra information so that the role play can become more authentic. It is then repeated. This is followed by writing down the development of the dysfunctional interpretation, including the accompanying feelings. Then both therapist and patient try to make connections between these interpretations, feelings and the various accompanying modes. The therapist should make sure that interpretations related to the self, to the other person(s), and to the assumed view the other person had about the child are addressed. The patient is just as sad and powerless as when this event actually took place and she concludes: "My mother was short with me, therefore she thinks I'm an annoying child." This conclusion contributed to the formation of her abandoned child mode: "No one loves me." The therapist writes all of this on a board using the patient's actual words. The therapist may ask the patient to rate the believability (0 to 100) of these conclusions and write them next to each conclusion on the board.

Phase 2: Role switching

In phase 2, the therapist suggests that they switch roles. The patient then attempts to immerse into the other individual, while the therapist now plays the role of the child. In preparation for the role play, the therapist emphasizes that the patient must try to 'become' the mother as much as possible. They discuss a number of typical characteristics the mother (or other individual) possesses, as well as the situation the mother was in during this period of her life.

Sample of historical role play phase 2: Role switching

Nora plays the role of mother and is standing by the table, busy cleaning. The therapist is Nora at eight years old and has just come home from school.

T = N: Mum, they were bullying me at school again. They took my new pen and broke it.

P = M: (annoyed) I'm busy, I don't have any time for this.

T = N: But now it's broken and doesn't. ...

P = M: Not now! I already told you!

(Therapist/Nora walks away with a sigh. Patient/mother sighs)

After the role play both patient and therapist dwell upon the thoughts and feelings the patient is experiencing. During this discussion the therapist pays special attention to signs that the patient has changed her view about the reasons for the parent's behaviour.

Sample of discussing phase 2

P: I realized that I was too tired to listen to my daughter and that's why I was so short with her. But I didn't think she was annoying.

T: If you didn't think Nora was annoying, why did you sigh?

P: Because I was very tired. I find it exhausting taking care of four small children.

T: When you now look back at the assumptions you just made (pointing at the board), what would you like to change?

P: That my mother was tired because she had to take care of four young children and it was too much for her. That's why she was so uninterested in me.

This new understanding can lead the patient to a reformation of the original assumptions. "My mother was short and had no time for me, but this had nothing to do with me, but rather was due to her being overly tired." The therapist writes this new text under the original assumption.

The patient should also be encouraged to look at her own role in the situation from the perspective of the parent looking at the child and comment on what she notices. Perhaps the child withdrew very early so that the parent was not confronted with his or her dysfunctional behaviour.

Sample of reflection phase 2: Personal share

T: What did you notice about your daughter as a mother?
P: Nothing.
T: What do you mean 'nothing'?
P: She doesn't react to anything I say.
T: Do you have any idea why she doesn't respond?
P: My mother doesn't know, maybe because she's busy with other things, but I was so scared, I was scared she would go crazy if I bothered her.
T: Now we can add a bit to your original assumption. … I didn't push her because I thought she would break down and. …
P: and think I was even more annoying.

The therapist must explain that the child had no other options as she was completely dependent upon her parents, and seldom saw how 'normal' parents react. Usually there are other examples from the patient's past in which she was directly labelled as difficult and/or annoying, which reinforced the belief that she was difficult. It is not the purpose of this exercise to make the patient feel guilty about her behaviour after the fact (see 'Common Problems with Historical Role Play').

Phase 3: Rescripting

During the third phase, the therapist again asks the patient to play the role of the child, but to use the new information she has learned from the previous role plays and subsequent discussions. For example, the patient can be more assertive and even speak in a louder voice. As this is now a new situation, the therapist is required to improvise in his role of the other person to accommodate the new behaviour of the child.

Once this improvisation is believable to the patient, the therapist can move on to reflecting upon this entire process and further re-evaluations of the original assumptions.

Sample of historical role play phase 3: Trying out new behaviours

In preparation for this role play, the therapist emphasizes that it is now time for the patient to try out new methods for getting her mother's attention. The therapist plays the mother, stands next to the table and appears to be busy with cleaning and caring for the household. The patient plays Nora, eight years old, and has just come home from school.

P: Mum, they were bullying me at school again. They took my new pen and broke it.

T = M: (annoyed) I'm busy and don't have any time right now.

P: But it doesn't work any more and ... They also called me names and hit me.

T = M: Not now! I told you I am busy!

P: Mum, don't you hear me?! They hit me and I have a bruise on my arm.

T = M: (looks up tired and says shocked) What did you say about a bruise? What did your teacher say?

P: Nothing, she didn't see it.

T = M: This has got to stop. I can't leave here, but I'll ask Aunty Mia to go with you to school tomorrow and the two of you can talk to your teacher about it.

The therapist used his knowledge about the patient's personal history to improvise the situation of Aunty Mia helping out. Aunty Mia lived very close to Nora and her family and often helped out when Nora's mother needed extra help. Should the patient find this improvisation unrealistic, the therapist must try something different. The therapist and patient finally come to the following conclusion:

> "If I had been clearer and as strong as an adult, and had told my mother that I was being bullied daily and that my teacher did nothing about the whole situation, then my mother would have either helped me herself or asked my aunty to help me, despite the fact that my mother was very tired. She would have done something. I am worthy of being loved."

The goal of phase 3 is not to give the patient the idea that she should have done things differently, but rather for her to experience the fact that there are different possible interpretations and ways of dealing with this situation. By doing so, the role play can be applied to different, more current situations in her life. This will help to give Nora, for example, a better understanding as to why she does not like to feel left out by her colleagues at work. It will also become clearer to her that she should discuss this with the management at work.

Common problems with historical role play

Problems faced in the practice of historical role play are similar to those of imagery. The most important problems are the following:

The phase 1 role play is too complicated – If during the preparation a scenario for role playing is discussed involving many different scenes, the therapist must help the patient to shorten the role play. Together with the patient, they must choose which situation had the most influence on the development of the schema or mode.

The parent's role is too violent – During role play it is possible that the chosen scene involves too much violence. In this case, the therapist cannot play the role of the parent and it is better to work on this situation using imagery rescripting.

The patient cannot play the role of the other individual – The reasons as to why the patient is unable to play the role of the other person must be looked into further. If no clear reason can be found, it is helpful to re-explain the rationale behind role play. Ask the patient to make one more attempt before deciding that she cannot do it. A possible explanation is that she is required to play an individual who is aggressive. The therapist can choose to skip phase 2 and ask the patient to try a different behaviour in phase 3. Yet another possibility is to switch to imagery rescripting.

No new perspective on the parent's behaviour is possible – If there is no chance of changing the parent's behaviour because he/she actually did reject the child, the therapist must not continue to force this issue. In this case, third phase rescripting involves becoming angry and walking away or the subject can be addressed in imagery exercises.

The patient feels guilty after phase 3 because she did not react in this fashion during the actual situation – The therapist must explain that as a child it was impossible for her to have this type of reaction due to her circumstances as well as the lack of examples of other possibilities in her life.

Only once she became an adult was it possible, with the help of a therapist, to think up alternative reactions and try them out.

The therapist is concerned that he is making the child feel guilty about her past behaviour – This train of thought is a mistake on the part of the therapist. The patient cannot feel guilty about this period in her life as she was a child and unable to know what to do in this situation. The role play can put into perspective her personal role as well as the role of her parent(s). This can actually have a very cathartic effect on her personal feelings of guilt as well as on her feelings about her parent(s). The patient can come to the following conclusion: "When I was a child, I was easily frightened, but now that's no longer necessary. My mother's reaction to my fear was inappropriate because she was overwhelmed and overly stressed with taking care of a young family and a divorce." This will result in very different emotions than the thought "My mother didn't love me."

Role play of a current situation

Just as with the historical role play, recent situations can be acted out in three phases.

In role plays with current situations, the focus is not on the development of the patient's schemas, but rather on the way schemas are maintained by misinterpretations of the behaviour of others. In particular phase 2 involves role switching and offers the patient the opportunity to reinterpret the behaviour of others as well as the effects of one's own behaviour on the behaviour of others.

Sample of role play of a present situation

It was unclear to Nora why she got into arguments with her boyfriend when she was in the punishing mode. While in this mode she was very critical of him and he could not do anything right. After participating in a few role plays in which Nora played the role of her boyfriend, she developed a better understanding of the effects of her behaviour when she was in this mode. She further began to understand that his irritated reaction reinforced her punitive side (even he's against me). She became more and more aware of the negative cycle in which she became stuck. She discussed with her boyfriend the idea of having a time out of half an hour if this should happen again so that she could try to stop her punitive side.

As previously mentioned, historical role play is helpful in ambiguous situations in which the behaviour of another individual (generally the parent) is interpreted in a black-or-white manner. The present role play is similar to historical role play, only now the patient uses situations she is currently dealing with as opposed to events from her past. During each phase of role play, the therapist tries, together with the patient, to write down the dysfunctional interpretations as clearly as possible. The relationship between cognitive, behavioural and experiential techniques is more clearly present in these role play techniques than in that of imagery rescripting. This relationship remains strong in the following two-or-more-chair technique, which will be described in the following section.

Two-or-more-chair Technique

The different sides of the patient's personality are physically placed onto different chairs for the two-or-more-chair technique. This is useful for BPD patients who find it difficult to cut themselves free from their punitive or protective modes. It is also a useful method when there is a battle between old, dysfunctional schemas and new, healthy schemas. This is also referred to as a 'schema dialogue'.

First, the two-chair technique is discussed as it can be used for the punitive parent and the protector modes. Then, the multiple-chair technique that involves multiple modes is discussed.

Two-chair technique for the punitive parent

Should the patient appear to be stuck in the punitive mode during a session, the therapist must first clearly state this to the patient. Usually the patient is unaware of this fact. Because of this, the therapist must explicitly state, and verify with the patient, which mode is in play during the session. He then suggests that this mode be placed on a separate chair (see Table 5.5). The empty chair, where the patient was sitting, remains free for the abandoned child (Little Nora). At that moment she is unable to put her feelings into words.

First, the patient sits on the Punitive Parent chair and expresses all the punitive comments this mode has. The patient then sits on the original chair again and the therapist continues by making it clear to the punitive

Table 5.5 Two- and multiple-chair technique.

Two-chair technique			
Mode	*Placement of mode*	*Therapist*	*Patient*
Punitive parent	Empty chair	Coaches the patient as a healthy adult	Healthy adult
Punitive parent	Empty chair	Healthy adult	Abandoned child
Punitive parent	Other chair	Healthy adult	Punitive parent
Protector	Empty chair	Coaches the patient as a healthy adult	Healthy adult
Protector	Empty chair	Healthy adult	Abandoned child
Protector	Other chair	Healthy adult	Protector
Protector	Other chair	Abandoned child	First protector, then abandoned child
Multiple-chair technique			
Mode	*Placement of mode*	*Therapist*	*Patient*
Punitive parent and protector alternate	Two empty chairs	Coaches the patient as a healthy adult	Healthy adult
Punitive parent and protector alternate	Two empty chairs	Healthy adult	Abandoned child
Punitive parent and protector alternate	Two other chairs	Healthy adult	Punitive parent or protector
Punitive parent and protector alternate	Three other chairs	Healthy adult or abandoned child	Punitive parent or protector
Two-chair technique with schemas and coping strategies			
Mode	*Placement of mode*	*Therapist*	*Patient*
Schema	Other chair	Coaches the patient as a healthy adult	Healthy adult
Coping strategy	Other chair	Coaches the patient as a healthy adult	Healthy adult

parent that his presence is damaging to Little Nora. If this is successful, then the therapist asks Nora to go to the chair of Little Nora and tell him, in Little Nora's voice, what is bothering her.

When dealing with a punitive mode, which is entirely negative regarding the patient, the therapist acts in a very confident, even angry, manner to force the punitive mode into silence.

Example of two-chair technique with punitive parent

P: I overslept again yesterday, so I can pretty much forget my new job. I'm so stupid.

T: I hear you talking in a very negative way about yourself. I think that I'm hearing you punitive parent side. Is that correct?

P: It's just plain stupid to be late for your second day of work.

T: I don't think that you're stupid at all and I suggest that we put your punitive parent side onto a different chair.

(points to an empty chair)

Would you like to sit there and tell me what your punitive parent is saying?

P: If I have to.

(moves capriciously to the other chair)

OK, I'll say it again; I think it's just plain stupid to oversleep for a second time.

T: I don't think it's stupid and you're not helping Little Nora at all by being so negative about her.

P: (verbally attacking the therapist) She is stupid and she's never going to learn.

T: OK, go to your first chair and listen to what I say to your punitive mode. (in an angry voice) Stop immediately! You're continuing to belittle Little Nora and I won't have it! (in a soft voice to Nora) What is the punitive side saying now?

P: Yeah but she really is stupid, always causing problems, and being irresponsible …

T: (verbally attacking the punitive mode) Stop it! Leave Nora alone until you can be nice and helpful to her. As long as you are talking this bullshit I don't want to hear you again.

(patient is silent)

T: What is the punitive side saying now?

P: Nothing any more.

T: (in a friendly tone) Would Little Nora sit in this chair now? (he motions towards another chair) Now tell me, what was the reason you overslept?

P: (sadly) I was up half the night and when I finally fell asleep, I ended up sleeping through the alarm clock.

T: So you were up late and couldn't sleep, that's awful. Were you worrying about something?

Many patients find it very difficult to sit in the punitive parent's chair particularly when the therapist becomes angry at the mode. To prevent this, the patient returns to her own chair when the therapist really starts to fight the punitive parent and the therapist can talk to the empty chair (see Table 5.5), or the patient only tells what the punitive parent says, whilst remaining in her own chair. As the therapist no longer receives a reply from the empty chair, he must ask the patient what the punitive parent would say when he talks to the empty chair and react based on this information. In this manner the patient continues to tell what the punitive parent says. At the same time this allows the patient to be a spectator to the battle between the therapist and the punitive parent.

Example of the two-chair technique with the punitive parent in an empty chair

The previous dialogue now continues in a different manner:

T: I don't think that you are stupid at all and I suggest that we put your punitive parent side onto a different chair. (He points to an empty chair.)

Would you like to sit there and tell me what your punitive parent is saying?

P: No I don't want to do that because I think you're going to get angry at me.

T: OK, then we'll sit the punitive side into an empty chair and I'll talk to the empty chair, is that OK with you?

(patient nods)

> T: (to the empty chair) You think that Nora is stupid to oversleep for a second time. I don't think it's stupid and you're not helping Little Nora by being so negative about her.
>
> T: (looks at the patient and asks in a friendly tone) What does the punitive side say now?
>
> P: That you don't understand it at all and that I *am* stupid.
>
> T: (in an angry tone to the empty chair) Stop it this instant! You're continuing to belittle Little Nora and I won't have it!
>
> (The therapist continues until the patient tells him that the punitive side is silent. Then he continues to talk to Little Nora.)
>
> T: Now tell me, what was the reason you overslept?
>
> P: (sadly) I was up half the night and when I finally fell asleep, I ended up sleeping through the alarm clock.
>
> T: So you were up late and couldn't sleep, that's awful. Were you worrying about something?

The patient can also fight the punitive side herself, changing chairs and successively playing healthy adult and punitive sides (Young, Klosko and Weishaar, 2003). However, we suggest only using this method when the patient can successfully play both the healthy adult and the punitive parent modes. The role of the therapist must then be limited to that of coaching the healthy adult. Often the problem is that the patient cannot formulate the words for the healthy adult and therefore needs coaching. But more often, and especially in early phases of therapy, the two-chair technique with the therapist fighting the punitive side is used to temporarily silence the punitive mode. Patients feel protected and relieved after this exercise. The therapist can then use the rest of the session to comfort and help the patient as long as the punitive parent remains silent. He is also in a better position to then help the patient with her problems.

Problems with using the two-chair technique with the punitive parent

There are times when the patient simply cannot tolerate the therapist's anger with the punitive parent, even when the chair remains empty. The punitive parent is after all a part of the true parent and some patients feel that fighting the punitive side will result in losing the whole parent, an idea that they cannot tolerate, despite the abuse and mistreatment that the parent may have caused. The therapist must then explain that the technique is about silencing that punitive part of the parent which is detrimental for the patient. This is not that she must totally reject her parent(s). Often psycho-education as to what a normal parental response is to a child's mistake is helpful. The therapist further explains that one learns more from making mistakes if they are accepted than when one is humiliated for making mistakes. In this way the patient learns why the therapist felt the punitive parent's reactions were so exaggerated and damaging. A possible compromise is that the therapist uses a less angry tone when dealing with the punitive parent. Nevertheless, it is his job to ensure that the punitive parent remains inactive, otherwise this mode will continue to command the patient's feelings. Despite the patient's resistance it might be necessary to be very firm in sending the punitive mode away. A symbolic action which is often helpful, is to put the empty punishing parent chair outside the room.

The two-chair technique with the detached protector

While the therapist's tone may be more neutral when dealing with the detached protector (see Chapter 9), his purpose remains the same, that is, ensuring that the mode, in this case the protector, retreats so that he can continue the therapeutic session with Little Nora in the other chair (see Table 5.5).

Example of the two-chair technique with the protector

T: So how are you doing today?

P: (in a flat tone) Good.

T: How was your week, did anything happen that you want to talk about?

P: (looks away and yawns) No, not really.

T: So everything's fine.

P: Yeah, maybe we could have a short session today.

T: I think that you are really in the protector mode today.

P: No, what do you mean? Everything's just OK with me.

T: You called me earlier this week saying that things were not so good with you and yet now you keep telling me that everything's OK. That's why I think you're in the protector mode. I suggest we put it in the other chair so that we can try to set it on the sidelines.

P: But I'm not in the mood to sit in the other chair. I'm way too tired.

T: May I then say something to the protector in an empty chair?

P: Fine with me.

T: (to an empty chair) I know that you're here for a reason, because some nasty things have happened this week. But I would like you to give me the chance to talk to Little Nora.

P: That's not going to help.

T: (to the empty chair) I can see that you're having trouble leaving and letting Little Nora deal with her unpleasant feelings, but I am here to help her out. So I would like to ask you to let me connect to Little Nora, if only for the rest of this session. I understand you are necessary to protect Little Nora from becoming desperate when she is all alone and feels bad. But now I am here to help Nora and therefore I would like to ask you to step aside, just for the moment, so that I can take care of Nora. I care about her and I would really like to help her with her feelings, but I cannot do that if you don't let me through.

(The therapist continues with this until he is able to have the space to talk with Little Nora.)

Problems with using the two-chair technique with the detached protector

In practice, there is really only one major problem with this technique, that is, when the detached protector refuses to retreat. Despite the fact that the detached protector is being difficult, it is important that the therapist does not become angry with the protector. Should he do this, he runs the risk of activating the punitive parent. On the other hand, the protector can be so stubborn that the therapist must become stronger in his dealings with this mode. Should this then result in activating the punitive parent, the therapist should give priority to addressing the punitive mode, putting it in a separate chair. In that case, there is a chair for the punitive mode, for the detached protector mode and for Little Nora. Although the therapist talks to the detached protector in this technique, it is important that he simultaneously talks to Little Nora in a tone of voice that is appealing to the Little Child mode ("I care for Nora and I know she is there behind the wall you have raised, and that she needs me to talk about her feelings …"). This will often motivate patients to lower their detached protector and to start to talk about their feelings. As soon as the patient starts to talk about her feelings, the technique has succeeded and the therapist addresses the patient's feelings and needs.

The therapist can even take the chair of Little Nora and express her needs; that is, to be able to express her feelings and to receive understanding and reassurance from the therapist. He also states that, while the protector does protect Nora, he does not teach her anything which will help her to solve her problems. In fact the protector interferes with Nora's development by not allowing her to feel anything at all.

A more cognitive technique, addressing motivation for letting the therapist bypass the detached protector, is discussing the advantages and disadvantages of the protector with Nora (see Chapter 9, 'Treatment Methods for the Protector').

Multiple-chair technique

Every now and then, the punitive mode will leave, but it is immediately replaced by the protector or vice versa. Because of this, another chair can be placed for the other mode. While this may appear to be the beginning of a child's party game, as long as the therapist does not lose sight of the goal of these chairs (contact with Little Nora), he should be able to manage them. Keeping in mind the need to keep the lines of communication with the little child open, the therapist can add a third chair to allow the needs of the abandoned child to be expressed (see Table 5.5).

This technique has the effect of giving the patient more insight into how her feelings, thoughts and behaviours are influenced by her different modes. She will also notice that these dialogues will become more and more a part of her own internal thought processes. Nora had previously spoken about the 'arguments in her head'. She has learned from her therapist that it is helpful to ignore the punitive parent in her head or to let go of the protective mode. The advantage for the therapeutic process is that she rejects the dysfunctional, while at the same time embracing the desired healthy adult side more. In any case, the therapist does not play the part of either the punitive parent or the detached protector as that would be confusing for the patient.

It is usually not sufficient to get rid of the punitive and/or protective modes only once, as they will reappear for a long time in subsequent sessions. Often the therapist will notice this based upon the tone of the patient's voice when she talks about herself. As soon as he notices a change in her intonation, he should ask if the relevant mode is at play. He should also request that she gives this mode its own chair and repeat the previously mentioned process.

Two-or-more-chair technique with changing schemas and coping strategies

During the final phase of therapy, these techniques can also be applied to dysfunctional schema and/or coping strategies that continue to cause problems. The problematic schema or coping strategy is placed into one chair and the healthy adult in the other. The patient can sit in either chair while the therapist coaches her as a healthy adult.

Experiencing and Expressing Emotions

BPD patients must learn to experience strong negative emotions without running away from them or behaving impulsively. Should the patient appear to not be able to experience emotions (see Chapter 2, 'The Detached Protector' and Chapter 9), it is important to explain why emotions are a necessary, healthy and functional part of human life. In doing so, the therapist explains not only that a feeling is an emotion, but also that these emotions evoke certain physical symptoms. In teaching the patient to understand emotions, he begins by explaining the most basic emotions: fear (and anxiety), anger (and rage), sadness (and dejection), happiness (and joy) and disgust. Exposure techniques as used in behavioural therapy, as well as writing letters to persons who have maltreated the patients (without sending them) (Arntz, 2004), can be helpful in inducing and learning to tolerate and accept emotions.

When cognitive diaries are used, describing emotions that are evoked in certain situations is essential (see Chapter 6 and Appendix B). As learning to deal with anger is a particularly difficult issue for BPD patients, a separate section has been dedicated to this subject.

Anger

Feeling and expressing anger (Angry Nora) is an exceptionally difficult problem for BPD patients. A very small minority of BPD patients start therapy being angry with everyone and everything, including their therapist. However, most patients hold back their anger as experience has taught them that when they express it, they face very serious consequences. Every now and then there is an outburst of unexpected and uncontrollable anger. This generally serves to reinforce the patient's fear of expressing anger even more.

If, in the session, the patient is to express her anger from the standpoint of her angry child, the therapist must stimulate this. He must be very careful in how he reacts to her anger. If he is too understanding, this will temporarily subdue her anger. On the other hand, should he take this outburst of resentment personally, he will react with his own punitive mode. Thus, again reinforcing the patient's belief that the expression of anger will be met with disapproval. He will also prematurely subdue her anger should he be too quick to defend himself. He best serves his patient by first allowing her the space to express anger about everything that is bothering her. In a neutral tone he must continue to ask her what she is angry at, why she is angry and whether or not there are more things she is angry about. Only once she has had the opportunity to express all her anger can the therapist begin to empathize with her and acknowledge her right to become angry. Only then can the connection between the anger and the angry child mode be made. Meanwhile, the patient will calm down a bit and her therapist can discuss the realistic and unrealistic components of her story. Because she has not learned how to deal with her anger in an appropriate manner for the future, it is helpful to try different options in role playing. In Table 5.6 we summarized four different facets that are related to anger.

Table 5.6   Expressing anger.

1. Venting anger	The therapist remains neutral and continues to ask questions.
2. Empathizing	The therapist empathizes with her animosity and makes connections to the modes.
3. Reality testing	Discussing what parts of the patient's anger are justified and what parts are not.
4. Practising assertive behaviour	Using role play to practise how better to deal with a similar situation in the future.

Example of dealing with anger

P: You don't understand anything. I don't know why I keep coming here. I called your secretary this morning to ask what time my appointment was and that stupid woman told me the wrong time. So I've had to sit in your boring waiting room for an hour.

T: (in a neutral tone) I can hear that you're angry at my secretary and at me because I don't understand you. Is there anything else you're angry about?

P: Yes there is. You have no idea how boring your waiting room is. There's no sunlight and only old magazines. And the people in there are nasty. They don't even bother to say hello.

T: (in a neutral tone) So you're angry at me because you had to sit in the waiting room for an hour and you don't like the people in there. Is there anything else that you're angry at?

P: I had an argument with my kids this morning. They didn't want to get out of bed again and were late for school. I ended up swearing at them as they left for school.

(And so on until all of her anger is out. The therapist continues to gather as much information as possible about why the patient is angry and then begins to speak in an empathetic tone.)

T: I can understand that you became angry. It was stupid of me not to write our appointment in my secretary's agenda. I can understand that Little Nora must have felt abandoned and now feels like she can't trust me.

P: I thought that *even you* can't be bothered with me and that you would do this right before your holidays …

(The therapist then thoroughly discusses the patient's feelings about the therapist's forthcoming vacation. This is followed by discussing the situations in which she expressed her anger in an inappropriate manner – when she swore at her children for being late – and the therapist teaches her how to express her anger more adequately in these situations, for example, by using role play.)

There are patients who do not dare to show any angry emotions. They rationalize these feelings away because of their fear of losing control and the consequences of this uncontrolled anger. The therapist tries to explain that it is this anger hoarding that causes the unexpected and uncontrollable outbursts of anger at the wrong time and (usually) directed at the wrong person. In this case, the therapist can function as model by showing the patient how to verbally express different degrees of anger, from hitting pillows via stomping his feet to telling the right person what you are angry about. He then asks the patient to do this with him. If she has trouble feeling anger, yet has the physical symptoms of anger, it is helpful to ask her to concentrate on these physical feelings. Each individual experiences different phenomena when repressing anger but some of the more common symptoms are stomach ache, headaches and tense muscles. Some patients may even clearly make fists in anger and not even realize they are doing so. The therapist can ask the patient to concentrate all of her attention on the tense part of her body or pain. He then, together with the patient, investigates what these feelings mean. If she either acknowledges or recognizes these feelings, they can discuss how to further deal with them as well as allowing as much expression of them as possible. The therapist suggests that the patient practises expressing mild anger/irritation both during and outside of therapy as much as possible. This will help her to avoid hoarding these feelings. In doing this she also experiences the reactions from the 'opposing' individual and generally speaking this is not as bad as she expected. More importantly, she realizes that by expressing anger at appropriate times, the chances of uncontrollable explosions of anger are greatly reduced. Another exercise is for the patient to tolerate these feelings and not immediately act them out. In doing so, she realizes that not only do these feelings dissipate in time, but she also learns more about maintaining control while experiencing strong emotions.

Experiencing and expressing other emotions

BPD patients often also fear losing control and becoming overwhelmed by other emotions such as fear, sadness or joy. To discover which feelings are aroused, just as previously described with anger, she can concentrate on her physical symptoms to identify them. For example, shallow, quick breathing accompanied by gripping the armrests of her chair can indicate that she is repressing fear or sadness. By gradually allowing these feelings into the session she will discover that they are in fact manageable and she can also try to do this outside of the therapy sessions. This can be done by consciously listening to certain types of music or watching emotional movies.

It will take a long time before she is able to show these feelings to anyone else besides her therapist. Sometimes she can also try to show them to a close friend or her children. Only once she has reached the point where her healthy adult is developed and she has developed relationships with other healthy adults is it advisable to practise these techniques outside of the safety of the therapeutic setting or good relationships.

Example of concentrating on physical symptoms in order to acknowledge feelings and naming them

Nora would like to apply to work as a volunteer, but she is not succeeding. Her therapist analyses why this is the case. Nora seems to think that they simply don't want her. The therapist asks her how this makes her feel.

P:　I don't know how I feel.

T:　Do you notice anything different in your body?

P:　Yeah, my stomach hurts.

T:　Concentrate on the pain in your stomach.

P:　I don't know if I can.

T:　Perhaps it would help if you put your hand where it hurts.

P:　(does this) It just gets worse.

T:　Just give it a try and try to concentrate on the pain and think about what this pain means.

P:　I think that I'm actually really scared. Sometimes I get stomach aches when things are difficult. Yeah, I'm scared that they're going to take advantage of me if I work there.

T:　So it appears that the stomach ache is a signal that you're scared.

(patient nods)

T:　That means that a stomach ache is a signal for you to try and find out what is scaring or bothering you.

Letter writing

The patient can learn to express her feelings by writing letters. This technique is often used in dealing with traumas, but can also be adapted to expressing emotions in different situations. The patient writes a letter addressed to the person(s) who have caused her pain in which she expresses all of her feelings of despair and/or anger. In general, this letter is never sent. This technique is not limited to negative feelings but can also be used to help the patient learn to express positive feelings. When she reads these letters aloud during her sessions, she is again helped to face these feelings.

She may also choose to write letters (or e-mails) to the therapist about subjects she feels unable to put into words during sessions. The therapist can use these letters as a vehicle to investigate why she cannot talk about these subjects. Perhaps the protector is involved in safeguarding her from strong emotions. On the other hand, the punitive parent may feel that some subjects must remain secret. Another possibility is that the abandoned child is ashamed. By treating the involvement of the modes, the patient can learn to discuss these emotions at a later stage of therapy and the need to write letters becomes less.

In this chapter, the different techniques have been directed at feeling, the so-called experiential techniques. By using these techniques the patient can manage (express feelings more and/or more adequately) and interpret her feelings differently. Because of this, these techniques are an important part of ST. However, it is important that these techniques are connected to the channels of both thought and action (see Table 3.1) so that the patient can put her altered insight into different behaviours.

Chapter 6 describes how cognitive techniques add to the patient's self-image as well as her views about others and the world as a whole.

6

Cognitive Techniques

Cognitive techniques can be used both to analyse and alter dysfunctional beliefs the patient has about both current and past events. In addition, the therapeutic relationship can also be analysed using these techniques (see Chapter 4, 'Cognitive Techniques and the Therapeutic Relationship'). Cognitive therapy as used in symptom-focused treatment is not an option for BPD patients during the first phase of therapy. However, it is possible for the patient to make connections between situations, feelings, thoughts and the associated modes (see Table 6.1). The therapist searches for connections between current situations and events in the patient's past. For example, the patient's abandoned child mode may cause her to panic at the mere thought that her boyfriend is leaving her with the dysfunctional belief that he will leave her forever. In this case, the therapist can explain the connections between this current situation and facts from her past, that is, when her mother did in fact leave the family for a few weeks without the children knowing why she had left or if she would return. This is not only an impossible situation for a young child to comprehend, but also a very frightening one for her as she is threatened in her existence. Because of this, each time the patient is faced with someone 'leaving' her, she is flooded with unexpected thoughts and feelings that relate to her memory of this important childhood event. However, these thoughts and feelings, while once appropriate to her childhood situation, are no longer appropriate in the present adult situation. The reactions of the angry child and the punitive parent modes can also be traced back to experiences from the patient's past. These

Schema Therapy for Borderline Personality Disorder. Arnoud Arntz and Hannie van Genderen
© 2009 John Wiley & Sons, Ltd.

Table 6.1   Cognitive diary for modes (see Appendix B).

SITUATION (What triggered my reaction?)
My boyfriend went to pick something up at a shop and came home an hour too late.

FEELING (How did I feel?)
Angry, panicky

THOUGHTS (What was I thinking?)
He's late again, he doesn't think about me at all. He doesn't love me.

BEHAVIOUR (What did I do?)
I kept checking to see if he was coming and kept calling his cellphone, which was
   turned off.

THE FIVE ASPECTS OF MYSELF
Which aspect was in play in this situation? Underline the aspects you recognize
   and describe them.
1. Protector:
2. Abandoned/abused child: *I was scared he wouldn't come back because he*
    doesn't love me any more.
3. Angry/impulsive child: *I was getting more and more angry because he couldn't*
    be bothered to call me and say why he was going to be late and he even had his
    phone turned off. He does that on purpose.
4. Punishing parent: *He's right to not love me any more, I'm an impossible person*
    to deal with.
5. Healthy adult:

JUSTIFIED REACTION (Which part of my reaction was justified?)
He's never late, so I was right to be concerned.

OVERREACTION (Which reactions were too strong?)
In which ways did I overreact or misread the situation?
I overreacted by thinking that he doesn't love me anymore, because I didn't know
   why he was late.
What did I do that made the situation worse?
My abandoned child side kept calling him and because I couldn't get through to him
   I became more and more panicked.

DESIRED REACTION
How would I like to be able to deal with this situation?
As he's usually on time and not late, there must be a good reason for being late.
   I only need to get angry if it turns out that he didn't think of me.
What could I do to help solve this problem?
I could try to distract myself by doing something else other than just waiting and
   worrying. If he's still not there in an hour, I could call the police or the hospital.

FEELING
Less anger and fear

---

explanations of connections to her past situation can be very helpful in her understanding as to why she is so often faced with uncontrollable emotions from one moment to the next.

After using experiential techniques it is helpful to have a cognitive analysis of the situation to bring structure to the experience on a cognitive level. In the description of historical role play this is explained in detail (see Chapter 5, 'Historical Role Play').

Once therapy has progressed to the point that the patient is capable of addressing her dysfunctional cognitions without being overwhelmed by negative emotions, the therapist can begin to teach her how to recognize the various nuances of thoughts using cognitive techniques. Beginning to teach these techniques too early on in therapy can result in the patient experiencing them as punishing or pointless. When the therapist finds the patient able to fill in the remainder of the cognitive diary for the different modes (Table 6.1 and Appendix B), the two of them can begin to challenge the patient's dysfunctional thoughts using a Socratic dialogue (see next section) and an experiment (see Chapter 7). The most common cognitive disputation techniques are often not adequate for BPD patients. In the example given in Table 6.1, the differences between justified reactions and overreactions can often only be put into words once one of the more complex disputation methods has been used (see further discussion). The therapist and patient write these challenges down as additional information in the cognitive diary for modes. In using this method, different types of cognitive diaries can be used. More information on cognitive diaries is available in general literature about cognitive therapy.

The following are common cognitive distortions that can dominate the patient's thought processes:

Overgeneralization – This is when one thinks that if something happens 'one' time it will always happen. The patient can think, for example, that if she makes a mistake, whatever she is doing will never work and that she is a failure.

Emotional reasoning – This involves basing conclusions about oneself and others on how one feels. For example, a patient concludes that the therapist cannot be trusted because she feels uncomfortable during sessions.

Personalization – The failure or success a patient experiences involves far too much of her own personal involvement, despite the fact that in reality her involvement is limited. An example of personalization is a patient who thinks that the death of a close friend is the patient's fault, when in fact the friend died of a serious disease.

Bad luck does not exist – The patient thinks that accidents and coincidences do not exist. She thinks that everything is thought out and takes place on purpose. In this manner of thinking, mistakes become lies and forgetting something becomes an example of betrayal. One who makes mistakes and/or has setbacks, deserves to be punished. If someone makes a mistake he deserves punishment and not understanding (there is no room for understanding). An example of this is the patient thinking that it is her fault she arrived late to an interview despite the fact she left on time but was delayed due to a flat tyre.

Thinking in black and white – This is when the patient can only think in terms of everything or nothing. People are good or bad, something is true or false, any other possible explanations simply do not exist. For example, the patient may think that someone who is unemployed has no value.

Thinking like this particularly stimulates the actions of the punitive parent mode and/or the protector. This reasoning can be disputed in a cognitive diary or during the session with the help of a Socratic dialogue in combination with complex cognitive techniques described below.

The most important cognitive problem with BPD patients is that they have the tendency to think in terms of black and white. This often leads to solutions that are not well thought out and brings along with it many conflicts as well as strong emotions.

Cognitive techniques, which help to develop a more nuanced manner of thinking, are of great help in adapting black-and-white thinking.

The most important techniques in training an individual to think in a more nuanced manner are evaluation on a visual analogue scale, multidimensional evaluation, the pie chart, two-dimensional reproductions of a supposed connection, the court house and historical testing. Different manners in which to encourage healthy views and to strengthen healthy schemas are flashcards and making a positive logbook. All techniques will be described briefly as elaborate descriptions of these techniques can be found in, among others, Arntz and Bögels (2000), Beck (1995), van Oppen and Arntz (1994), Padesky (1994) and Sprey (2002).

The Socratic Dialogue

In order to discover which reactions are justified and which reactions are too strong, the therapist and patient can discuss her thoughts with the help of a Socratic dialogue. A Socratic dialogue between patient and therapist involves allowing the patient to discover that there is more than one possible interpretation for a given event. During this dialogue the therapist makes frequent use of open questions, beginning with the words 'who', 'what', 'when', 'where', 'why' and 'how'. His goal is to encourage the patient to think about her dysfunctional thoughts.

Examples of commonly asked questions are:

– How do you know that?
– What facts support this argument; which oppose it?
– How does that work?
– How many times has that happened?
– What do the people in your general surroundings think about this?
– Imagine that this actually does happen, what is really so bad about this?
– If this does happen, what could you do about it?

To successfully participate in a Socratic dialogue the patient must have sufficiently developed her healthy adult mode. This is necessary for her to be capable of thinking up alternative interpretations. This is one of the main reasons that BPD patients are not capable of a Socratic dialogue during the first stage of therapy. Only once the healthy adult mode has become stronger can the therapist give the patient homework assignments such as filling in the cognitive diary, defying difficult situations and attempting alternative interpretations (see Table 6.2). Upon completing the cognitive diary in Table 6.2, the patient can continue to fill in Table 6.3. However, this is not necessary if the alternatives have become clear to her.

Evaluation on a Visual Analogue Scale

When a patient thinks only in terms of black and white about herself and others, she can be taught to appreciate different nuances on a visual

Table 6.2   Cognitive diary for modes (also see Appendix B).

EVENT (What triggered my reactions?)
My girlfriend said that she didn't like it when I left her waiting for half an hour.

FEELING (How did I feel?)	Strength of feeling
Scared	80

THOUGHT(S) (What did I think?)	Believability
	90

She doesn't like me anymore and will break off contact.

BEHAVIOUR (What did I do?)
I shut up and didn't say anything.

THE FIVE ASPECTS OF MYSELF
Which aspect was in play in this situation? Underline the aspects you recognize and describe them.
1. Protector: *Could not deal with the thought of losing her and made me pull away.*
2. Abandoned/abused child: *Fear of abandonment.*
3. Angry/impulsive child:
4. Punishing parent: *You do everything wrong.*
5. Healthy adult:

DISPUTATION OF THOUGHTS (Ask critical questions about your thoughts.)
Indications that my girlfriend no longer likes me and will break off contact:
   She said that she didn't like it that I left her waiting.
   At first she didn't believe that there was nothing I could do about it because my mother called and began to complain about everything. We didn't make a new appointment to see each other.

Indications that my girlfriend does like me:
After we finished talking about my being late, she was friendly like she usually is. When we said goodbye, she said that we should see each other again soon.

What would someone else say about this?
That I shouldn't make such a big deal out of it because I've known her for four years and in previous situations when she was angry with me she didn't break off our friendship.

ALTERNATIVE THOUGHTS
It was logical that I didn't like her criticism, but I don't need to assume the worst in this kind of situation.

Table 6.3   Continuation of cognitive diary for modes (also see Appendix B).

JUSTIFIED REACTION
It was unpleasant to be criticized and it is a good thing that I apologized.

OVERREACTIONS (Which reactions were too strong?)
How did I overreact or see things wrong?
I overreacted by thinking that she didn't like me anymore and that she would break off our friendship.

What did I do to make matters worse?
The protector made sure that I severed contact and because of that the evening wasn't as nice as it could have been.

DESIRED REACTION (How would you like to be able to deal with this situation?)
It was logical that I didn't like her criticism, but I don't need to assume the worst.

What would be a better way of dealing with this situation?
I could have said to her that I was having trouble dealing with it and what I was really afraid of, then we could have talked about it.

FEELING
Relief

analogue scale. This scale goes from one extreme (i.e. stupid) to the other extreme (i.e. smart). The therapist draws a line on a board or a flip chart and writes 'stupid' (0) on the left, and 'smart' (100) on the right. If the patient thinks that she is 'stupid' the therapist asks her to place herself somewhere on this scale. In other words, to what degree does she believe that she is 'stupid'. Generally speaking, she will choose 0 or close to 0. He follows this by asking the patient to place other people she knows on this same scale. Finally he asks her to again find a place for herself on this scale. He encourages her to first find two examples of extremes (i.e. a very smart/ stupid person) and then to place different individuals between these extremes (see Figure 6.1). This way, she discovers that, contrary to what she thought when starting the exercise, she does not belong at the extreme ends of the scale. Nora completed the highest level of high school (in the Netherlands there are different levels of high school: VMBO (lower and average), HAVO (higher) and VWO (pre-university)) and in the end placed herself in the middle.

```
          L    C    Nora  A    X
  0 ----x ------x--------x------x-------x------- 100
  Stupid                                    Smart
```

L: mentally handicapped cousin
C: friend who completed (lower) high school
A: friend at university
X: Nobel Prize winner

Figure 6.1   Example of a visual analogue scale.

Multidimensional Evaluation

Should the patient gauge her self-image or her image of others in one dimension (e.g. I'm not nice because I have no friends), then the therapist can, together with the patient, make an inventory of what other characteristics make a person worthy. They can also make an inventory of characteristics that make a person unworthy. The patient will no doubt name dimensions that 'prove' that she is not nice (e.g. no friends; difficultly making social contacts and fear of speaking in social situations). The therapist should write these dimensions down, while at the same time stimulating the patient to try and think of more dimensions for the 'nice' category. He does this by asking her what she finds 'nice' about others and then to think about which characteristics make a person 'nice' (or 'not nice'). Once enough characteristics and/or dimensions have been found, these are also placed onto a visual scale with 0 being one extreme (when the characteristic is completely absent) and 100 being the other extreme (when the characteristic is absolutely present) (see Figure 6.2). This is followed by the patient again placing people she knows on these dimensions (Figure 6.3). The last part of this method involves the patient evaluating herself on these different dimensions (see Figure 6.4). The therapist can influence the individuals the patient chooses to evaluate by also suggesting people from the popular media who the patient does not personally know but who are known publicly as being not nice (e.g. serial killers or war criminals). When this method is successfully applied, the patient will end up with a much more nuanced and positive image of herself than she started out with (see Figure 6.4).

1. Making an abstract concept concrete

```
0/ -------N---------------------------------------------------------/100
nice      Nora                                  not nice

0/ ---------------------------------------------------------------/100
no friends                                      many friends

0/ ---------------------------------------------------------------/100
cannot get along                                can get along
with anyone                                     with everyone

0/ ---------------------------------------------------------------/100
will not do                                     will do anything
anything for others                             for others

0/ ---------------------------------------------------------------/100
cannot work                                     works well
with others                                     with others

0/ ---------------------------------------------------------------/100
always in a bad                                 never in a bad mood
mood
```

etcetera

Figure 6.2   Thinking up different dimensions.

2. Place others on these scales (including extreme cases, e.g. public figures)

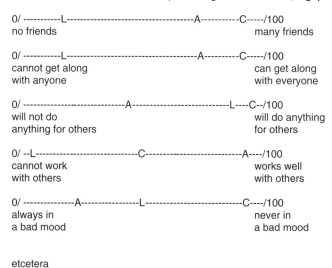

```
0/ ----------L----------------------------------A----------C-----/100
no friends                                      many friends

0/ ----------L----------------------------------A---------C-----/100
cannot get along                                can get along
with anyone                                     with everyone

0/ -------------------------A---------------------------L----C--/100
will not do                                     will do anything
anything for others                             for others

0/ --L--------------------------C---------------------------A----/100
cannot work                                     works well
with others                                     with others

0/ --------------A----------------L--------------------------C---/100
always in                                       never in
a bad mood                                      a bad mood
```

etcetera

Figure 6.3   Placing others on a dimension.

3. Let the patient score herself on the scales

```
0/ -----------L-------N----------------------------A-----------C-----/100
no friends                                        many friends
```

```
0/ -----------L------------------------------------A------N--C-----/100
cannot get along                                  can get along
with anyone                                       with everyone
```

```
0/ --------------------------------A----------------------N--L----C--/100
will not do                                       will do anything
anything for others                               for others
```

```
0/ --L----------------------------C----N----------------------A----/100
cannot work                                       works well
with others                                       with others
```

```
0/ --------------A-----------------L--------N-----------------C----/100
always in a                                       never in a
bad mood                                          bad mood
```

4. Translate the conclusion to the first scale

```
0/ --------------------------L--A----------N-------------C-------/100
nice                          NORA              not nice
```

Figure 6.4   Placing yourself on a dimension.

Two-Dimensional Reproductions of Supposed Connections

When the patient thinks that two factors are logically connected, one can test this theory to see if there are actual correlations between these two factors. In this case, two-dimensional reproductions are the most useful. The dysfunctional thought that 'success at work leads to happiness' was a reoccurring subject with Nora during therapeutic sessions. If the statement is true that 'the more successful one is at work, the happier he/she is', all of the individuals should have a position near the diagonal line in Figure 6.5.

When the patient tried to place as many people as possible in this two-dimensional space, the previously assumed correlation became less clear than she originally thought. She began to realize that happiness must be based on factors other than success at work. In fact the only individual who

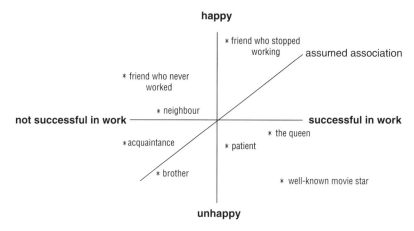

Figure 6.5 Two-dimensional representation of an assumed association between happiness and success with work.

ended up directly on the diagonal line was her brother who was addicted to heroin and had never worked.

Pie Chart

A pie chart can help visualize the level of influence that an event or characteristic has on the whole.

This method is particularly helpful with BPD patients who have a tendency to overestimate their own personal level of involvement (or fault) in various situations that go wrong. First, the patient must think of which individuals and aspects influenced the given situation or played an important role in the situation. The therapist encourages her to think of as many different aspects as possible. After this, he asks her to give each person or aspect a part of the 'blame' in the pie chart. Next, all the percentage parts are drawn in the circle as parts of the pie. The patient places her pie part last and discovers that she is not fully to blame; contrary to what she first thought when she rated her share 100% (see Figure 6.6). Putting the patient's contribution into perspective has the additional effect that the punitive parent side is weakened.

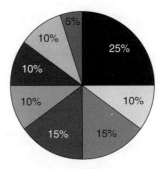

1. Mother was an alcoholic and did nothing   (25%)
2. He had a serious problem with his intestines   (10%)
3. Child protective services reacted too late   (15%)
4. Her brother made several attempts at detoxification
which he messed up   (15%)
5. His friends were too late with calling the doctor   (10%)
6. The dealer sold him stronger drugs   (10%)
7. His girlfriend had just broken up with him and he
didn't want to live anymore   (10%)
8. The patient kicked him out after he stole money from   (5%)
her

Figure 6.6   Nora had a brother who died of an overdose of heroin when she was 16 years old. She was convinced that it was her fault because during that time in her life, she had to take care of her brothers and sisters. After making a list of exactly who and what else were responsible, she created this pie chart.

Courthouse Method

Another method of assigning 'blame' to or 'discharge' a person in a certain situation is the courthouse method. This is a form of role play in which the patient takes on the role of the prosecutor and the therapist plays the part of the lawyer who makes the arguments against the prosecutor. If this method works well, the roles can be switched so that the patient becomes the lawyer and the therapist becomes the prosecutor. Sometimes it is helpful to have the patient play the role of judge who makes the verdict after listening to the arguments of the prosecutor and the lawyer. This technique is similar to the two-chair technique (see Chapter 5); however, the courthouse technique is directed at dysfunctional thoughts while the two-chair technique is directed at modes.

Historical Testing

The patient's schemas were developed early on during her childhood. Because of this, her self-image has been distorted for the greater part of her life. Historical testing is a method of adjusting the incorrect image the patient has of herself based on her past experiences. Often BPD patients have the idea that they are bad and difficult and that they have always been this way. The therapist can test this theory by returning to each period of the patient's life, choosing the periods in a way that they more or less line up with normal developmental phases. The patient first collects information about normal child development for each developmental phase. Then, different materials such as photographs, tapes or videos, school reports, reports from child protective services and letters are analysed to either support or refute the argument that the patient has always been bad even when she was a child (see Appendix D). Here it is particularly important to deal with the first few years of the patient's life. Many patients think that they were bad from the moment they were born. By actually looking at baby photographs, therapist and patient can test this theory. Of course there is absolutely nothing to indicate that a baby in a photograph is a 'bad' child. School reports and such are carefully examined in the same manner with special attention given to the teachers' comments. When it is feasible, family, old neighbours, teachers and caregivers are also asked about the patient. Often the patient has a great deal of trouble doing this, as she is convinced that she will be confronted with proof that she truly is 'bad'. This almost never happens in actual practice. Generally other individuals in the patient's environment knew that there was something wrong in the family, but found it difficult to intervene. All of this is very helpful in creating a more nuanced self-image for the patient. She often develops more understanding for the small child that she once was. By doing this she can see more clearly the strong role that her parent(s) and childhood traumas played in the development of her (later) problems. It becomes easier for her to send away her punishing mode as well as to offer more support to her abandoned child mode.

Flashcards

The punitive parent mode often rears its head each time the patient is faced with something unpleasant in her life. A flashcard serves as an aid to memory and can help her deal with the unpleasant situation. The patient writes on one side of the flashcard the viewpoint of the punitive parent ("I feel guilty, therefore it is my fault that everything went wrong. This is what my punitive parent says"). On the other side of the flashcard she writes her new, more refined/balanced/nuanced view ("I feel guilty, but that doesn't mean that I am guilty, because there could be other reasons as to why it didn't work out. It could be bad luck or perhaps someone else had something to do with it. Only once I really sit down and put everything into its proper place can I really know whether or not I am guilty. The punitive parent is exaggerating and I don't need this side right now").

Positive Logbook

Another way of strengthening the newly formed schemas is by means of a positive logbook. Individuals with a personality disorder have the tendency to be very selective in their memory and only remember experiences that reinforce their old, dysfunctional schemas. Because of this, patients must make use of their logbooks for a longer time and keep track of experiences and facts that oppose their old schemas and support new ones (see Appendix C). In the beginning patients require a great deal of support when using this method as they find it difficult to think of positive things. They forget to include small, daily situations such as cooking a nice meal or an hour at the gym, despite the fact that these contribute to a positive self-image. Most patients think that they can only write down a positive experience in their logbook if it is unusually good, such as getting a new job or taking care of someone who was sick for a whole week. So, writing an application letter for a job or doing the shopping for someone who is sick seldom warrants a place in their positive logbook. Patients also tend not to include situations in which their response was good; however, the result was not what they had wished (either by accident or due to the influence of others). For example, the patient may have told her boyfriend in a very appropriate manner that she did not like that he did not show up for their previous date. Her boyfriend then reacted in a rude manner and the patient became upset and felt that this situation should not be put in a positive logbook. It is then up to the therapist to explain that in such a situation the fact that she dared to say what she normally would not say is actually a positive action and should go into her positive logbook. If the patient is keeping a positive logbook, the therapist should ask her about it at each session. If he does not do this, her interest in the logbook will fade.

Together, cognitive and experiential techniques are a powerful means for procuring change. Although the chapter on cognitive techniques is relatively short in this book, this should by no means underestimate the importance of the cognitive work within this type of therapy. Therapists with no formal training in cognitive techniques will often miss the important skills in using ST. This is particularly evident with techniques such as verbalization, making concepts concrete and disputation of schemas as well as formulating healthy, new schemas. Most importantly the therapist must be able to transfer these techniques to his patient. She needs these techniques in order to refine her thinking, and to deal better with difficult situations in the future.

How exactly healthy thoughts can be translated into healthy behavioural patterns is described in Chapter 7 as well as in the section 'Behavioural Pattern-Breaking' in Chapter 10.

7

Behavioural Techniques

Behaviour does not change simply because the patient has developed new schemas. Thinking differently and feeling differently does not always automatically translate into behaving differently. In order to learn new behaviours, new skills must also be learned. Behavioural techniques can be used when the patient lacks the skills to translate new insights into new behaviour. The behavioural techniques used in the therapeutic relationship have been briefly discussed in Chapter 4.

For more in-depth explanations of these techniques, we refer the reader to the extensive body of literature on behavioural therapy as well as professional courses in behavioural therapy. The following is a summary of applicable techniques with short descriptions of their use. It is important to realize that these techniques are only useful when the patient is capable of using her healthy adult mode. When this mode is sufficiently developed, she will acknowledge that she has the right to her own opinions and needs. Attempting skills training too early, one will fail as the punitive parent mode and/or the protector mode will constantly interfere with the therapeutic process ("I can't do this either") and thwart the therapy. The therapist must encourage the patient to try her newly learned behaviours not only during the sessions, but also in everyday life (see Chapter 10, 'Behavioural Pattern-Breaking').

Schema Therapy for Borderline Personality Disorder. Arnoud Arntz and Hannie van Genderen
© 2009 John Wiley & Sons, Ltd.

Experiments

Experiments are the natural progression of cognitive therapy as they are a manner in which the patient can actively try out her newly acquired insights (see Appendix E).

When she comes to the conclusion that certain dysfunctional beliefs are incorrect, she may later begin to doubt again. Using experiments is one way to strengthen her new schemas while at the same time weakening her old schemas. The therapist and patient discuss what steps the patient should take to find out which of the two schemas is the most accurate. If the patient had the tendency to deal with situations from her protector mode and was not used to attending to her needs due to the fear that she would be rejected again (which happened to her often in the past), experimentation can focus on her learning to express her needs more often. Both therapist and patient prepare a number of concrete situations in which the patient can do this. Once she has completed these experiments, they can be evaluated.

Because of the patient's past and her lack of healthy experiences, it is often necessary to train her in healthy behaviours before beginning with experimentation.

Skills Training and Role Play

As previously mentioned, patients with BPD lack many of the social skills that most people take for granted, or they know them but habitually don't use them for themselves. This has a strong influence on how they express anger and seek affection. Before the patient faces a new situation, it is necessary to explain what the acceptable behaviour is for this situation and how you apply it. BPD patients often state that they raised themselves by watching others (outside of the family) and this was how they learned to deal with various social situations. This resulted in partially adequate or completely inadequate knowledge and utilization of social skills. By using social skills training and role play, these skills can be learned.

Social skills training and role play can be used as a means of preparing the patient for new situations. In this way her chances of developing new and better relationships are greatly increased and she learns how to behave differently in existing relationships. Daring to express her emotions and standing up for her needs are the main points of this method.

Problem Solving

Problem solving deserves special attention in treating BPD patients. These patients have the tendency to swing back and forth between being impulsive and being dependent when it comes to thinking of solutions for problems. Patients can learn to be less impulsive by practising adding a 'thinking break' into the problem solving process. By doing this, patients learn to solve problems by splitting them up into smaller parts. This is followed by thinking up different possible solutions for each individual part of the problem and writing down the pros and cons of each potential solution. The therapist encourages her to think up as many different solutions as possible. He encourages her not to disregard any possibilities because she is influenced by either the punitive parent or the protector. Only once a thorough assessment has been made to determine the most appropriate solution should the patient try it out and then evaluate it (see Appendix G).

Discussing Dangerous Behaviours

The discussion of dangerous behaviours is a recurring theme in therapy with BPD patients. At the beginning of therapy, topics include suicide attempts, self-injury (see Chapter 8, 'Suicide and Self-Injury') and substance abuse. This is followed by other topics, such as the patient engaging in damaging relationships, resulting in her returning to old, dysfunctional schemas. Keep pressing the patient to stop the damaging behaviour and discuss alternatives that will have a similar effect on her feelings of anxiety, restlessness and anger. For example, encouraging the patient to try alternatives such as a warm bath and a glass of milk instead of alcohol when she is stressed. In addition regular discussion of the connection between these behaviours and the different modes that influence the behaviour is also very important. This should be followed by applying the appropriate techniques. One should not expect a quick change in the patient's behaviour and not be surprised when the 'old' behaviours return when she is faced with an unpleasant situation.

Discussing New Behaviours

Discussing dangerous or damaging behaviours – or rather what the patient should not do – should always be coupled with discussing new behaviours. The new behaviours are the positive alternatives to dysfunctional behaviours and are feasible for the patient. There is little to be gained from advising the patient to avoid her boyfriend, who so blatantly neglected her, if no attention is given to the question of whom the patient should turn to for help and how she should ask for help. The patient has difficulty successfully assessing others while at the same time she also has the predisposition to pick the wrong individuals as a sort of confirmation of her own dysfunctional schemas. Only once the patient has developed a (strong) healthy adult side will her ability to judge others be improved.

The second half of therapy is geared towards helping the patient find an appropriate hobby, study or employment. Making new friends and developing close relationships (or relationship therapy) is part of this process. Creating new and more intimate relationships is particularly difficult for patients who were abused as children and are generally distrustful of others. The abandoned/abused child must practise gradually exposing more and more of herself. She needs support in learning to express her needs and showing affection towards friends. Physical affection such as a hug is often particularly threatening for BPD patients as their past experiences with this type of affection were often in connection with force, sex or punishment. Because of this, the therapist and patient carefully research which individuals can be trusted during this difficult behaviour-changing process. In using psycho-education and advising the patient, the therapist is much less constrained than in other forms of therapy. He does this from a reparenting perspective and looks to support what is best for the patient. Slowly he allows her more and more autonomy over her own life, in the same way that a parent gives a teenager more responsibility. Treatment is considered complete when the patient has built up a relatively strong social network and is involved in daily activities that are beneficial to her as a person.

Without applying behavioural techniques, the cognitive and experiential techniques often remain without grounding in the present life. The major fault with many therapies is that, while insight is developed, it is not actively put into use. Because of this, behavioural techniques are an indispensable part of ST as they put cognitive and experiential theory into practical use.

The following chapter focuses on a number of methods and techniques geared for specific situations.

8

Specific Methods and Techniques

Homework

BPD patients do not do homework in the 'usual' manner of homework assignments in behavioural therapy. This is usually more the result of inability than of unwillingness. Because of this, it is better to recommend rather than require homework, while accepting when the patient does not succeed. It may be interesting to look into which mode is influencing the patient not to do her homework. The therapist can use certain tools to help the patient to engage in homework and/or to report what interfered with doing it (e.g. see Appendix F). During the sessions following a homework assignment, it is important to ask the patient regularly about her homework assignments even if she does not bring this subject up. The contents of the homework should always be connected with what has taken place during the session and can be related to any of the following subjects:

Listening to taped sessions – At the beginning of therapy, the therapist asks the patient to always listen to the taped sessions. Although this may appear to be a very simple homework assignment in theory, the actual practice of it is not simple. The patient may be afraid that she has said the wrong thing or perhaps sounds strange, which may result in activating her punitive side. Because of this, she avoids the assignment as much as possible. At other times she does not dare to listen to a session during which strong or unpleasant emotions are involved when she is at home alone. The detached protector stops her from doing so out of fear she

Schema Therapy for Borderline Personality Disorder. Arnoud Arntz and Hannie van Genderen
© 2009 John Wiley & Sons, Ltd.

may experience an overflow of emotions while at home and without the support of her therapist. Or she is afraid of activation of the punitive mode. However, listening to these recordings can have a strong reinforcing effect of the therapy session. It is impossible to remember everything that took place during a session; therefore, re-listening to the session allows the patient to retrieve more information. In addition, a patient often only discovers the therapist's meaning upon re-listening to a taped session. Often this meaning is completely opposite to what the patient originally thought took place during the session (also see Chapter 3). Because of all of these reasons it is highly recommended that the therapist regularly enquires as to whether or not the patient is listening to the taped sessions. As therapy goes on, he can reserve asking about listening to taped sessions until after a particularly emotional session.

Making special tapes – The therapist can choose to make special tapes about specific subjects. Common subjects for tapes generally involve offering support to the abandoned child and refuting the punitive parent. The patient can then listen to these tapes as often as she finds necessary.

Reading flashcards in situations where they are appropriate (see Chapter 6).

Writing letters to individuals from the patient's past (and not sending them) (see Chapter 6).

Making a cognitive mode diary (see Chapter 6, 'The Socratic Dialogue' and Appendix B).

Keeping a positive logbook and if desirable asking the patient to read this aloud to herself (see Chapter 6 and Appendix C).

Meeting up with friends and asking for affection from others (see Chapter 7).

Relaxation and meditation exercises – The main reason therapists advise patients to do relaxation exercises is that they offer alternative forms of coping with strong emotions. They also have an added effect of replacing the need for the detached protector mode. There are many different types of relaxation and meditation exercises that are helpful in achieving this goal. The therapist should check whether the patient uses such techniques more to detach from emotions, which is actually a detached protector strategy, than to accept emotions, which is a healthy adult strategy.

Doing things that the patient enjoys or is good at – By participating in activities that she is either good at or simply enjoys, she experiences success and hopefully satisfaction. These experiences are helpful in fighting her punitive side. She also learns to discover her needs and to take care of herself. In other words, the healthy adult learns to take care of the patient.

Comforting – The patient must learn to comfort herself, if necessary, by means of a transitional object. This transitional object can be something she buys for herself (a stuffed animal) or something small that the therapist gives to her (a key ring or a card with something positive about the patient written on it).

Expressing anger about small issues (see Chapter 5, 'Anger').

Two-chair technique – The patient may try this technique at home (see Chapter 5).

Imagery rescripting – The patient may also try this at home. This is only advisable once the patient's healthy adult side has developed to the point at which she can support and comfort the abandoned child. Before the therapist suggests that she try this at home, it should have taken place successfully a few times during sessions. (However, the patient can practise in earlier stages with the help of an audio tape of an imagery rescripting during a session.)

Trying out new behaviours (see Chapter 7).

Trying out new activities, such as a new job, a new study or different social contacts (see Chapter 7).

Pharmacological Therapy

While there is not one pill that will cure BPD, there are a number of medications commonly prescribed for BPD patients. As these medications are commonly used we have a few comments on this subject. We often see BPD patients with unintentional results of pharmacological therapy such as addiction and medicine abuse. The prescribed medications are often used in combination with alcohol and/or over-the-counter medications (e.g. pain killers) for suicide attempts.

Antidepressive medication is useful in treating serious depressive symptoms. However, there is no convincing evidence that antidepressants are helpful for BPD, not even for the affective or impulsive problems these patients have (Stoffers *et al.*, 2008).

SSRIs may even hinder psychological treatment of BPD, although this should be rigorously tested (Giesen-Bloo *et al.*, 2006; Simpson *et al.*, 2004).

Should anxiety-reducing medication be indicated, we recommend neuroleptic agents over benzodiazepines. It is our experience that benzodiazepines actually heighten emotions during crises, when in fact they are prescribed to mute or numb these emotions. The risk of acting out and losing inhibition over behaviour and emotions increases rather than decreases, in particular when benzodiazepines are used in combination with alcohol. This often results in an increase of self-harm and/or suicide attempts. With patients that are affected the risks should be discussed including reasons to terminate the use of these kinds of medication. This will be done in close contact with the primary physician and psychiatrist. In general it is recommended that medication is used sparingly and for short periods of time. Learning to deal with one's emotions, as well as being open to receive support and understanding is impaired when the patient's emotions are numbed. The change brought about by experiential techniques is an essential part of therapy. Psychopharmacia subdue the emotional life and this is not helpful in bringing about deeper personality changes, which are the ultimate goals of ST. Preliminary empirical data indeed suggest that patients using medication have fewer benefits from therapy than patients not using medication (Giesen-Bloo *et al.*, 2005; Simpson *et al.*, 2004).

Crisis

During the beginning of treatment, BPD patients may experience episodic crises, as both objective and subjective factors can cause the patient to become overly upset. Most crises are caused because the patient makes things worse than they actually are. This is due to her dysfunctional schemas being unknowingly activated and the patient ending up in one of the dysfunctional modes. This is further exasperated by her fear of strong emotions and the punitive attitude towards needs and emotions.

The therapist must try to release the patient from these crises as quickly and often as possible. This is of extreme importance in strengthening the therapeutic relationship and is an excellent moment to change the modes. During a crisis, emotions that are normally suppressed by the protector during the sessions are openly expressed. The therapist has contact with the abandoned child during the crisis and can comfort and reassure her. Should the angry child be in the foreground, the therapist could give her the opportunity to vent her rage. The expression of emotions is encouraged and it is not advisable to look for practical solutions for the patient's problems at this time. It is of great importance that the therapist shows the patient that he can handle strong emotions and offers her support and comfort.

Example of handling a crisis

Nora calls her therapist in a panic because she is about to be evicted for not paying her rent, which was partially due to her room-mates.

T: I understand that you are shocked that your landlord is threatening to evict you. And you are angry that he suddenly walked into your flat. That makes perfect sense and is very understandable. Tell me the rest.

Nora tells the entire story. The therapist interrupts her every now and then to make short comments that reinforce his sympathy with her situation. Once she has calmed down he tries to make connections with the modes.

T: Now that I've heard the entire story I can understand why you feel so abandoned. The punitive side is no doubt arguing that this is your own entire fault, which is completely false. What you need is support. When you were young, you got yelled at when something bad happened to you, but that's not going to happen here.

P: But tomorrow I'll be out on the street with nowhere to go.

The therapist must suppress his impulse to look for a practical solution to this problem and continues to support her.

T: I understand that you don't know where you're going to go tomorrow because you're very upset. What did your room-mates say when the landlord was there?

P: They were pissed off and said that they would pay the rent back within a month.

T: Thank goodness you're not on your own! It's good to hear that you have support in this difficult situation.

If necessary the therapist offers an extra session or opportunity for phone contact later in the week in order to ensure that she receives the necessary support during this crisis.

The therapist tries to link what is going on now and the activation of one or more modes, as well as experiences from her past that may possibly play a role. Most importantly, the therapist must show the patient that he is there for her and will not abandon her. He must ensure that she does not hurt herself or others while in this panicked state. He further encourages her to find others in her circle of family/friends to support her emotionally. Only once she is calm does he attempt to find practical solutions. However, often the patient has already thought up solutions she is capable of following.

If the patient is intoxicated (e.g. pills or alcohol) or has attempted to kill herself, this method is not applicable and the help of qualified medical staff must be called into play. Should this be the situation, the therapist can only begin to analyse the crisis once it is finished.

Suicide and Self-Injury

When a patient expresses the desire to commit suicide or threatens to harm herself (self-injury), the therapist shifts all attention towards stopping this behaviour. Together with the patient, the therapist attempts to discover from which mode these suicidal or self-injury desires come. In general, each mode maintains different 'reasons' for self-injury or suicide attempts. The protector commits these behaviours as a way of suppressing strong emotions such as sadness and fear. It is as if the patient prefers physical pain to psychological pain. For her, the latter is unbearable. The punitive parent uses suicide and self-injury as a form of punishment for the patient's faults and shortcomings. The angry child shows the same behaviour in order to punish others around her for what they have done to her (see Chapter 9). After the therapist has determined which mode is at play, he then intervenes using the appropriate method for that given mode. Once these harmful behaviours have disappeared, he should begin each session by asking the patient if she still has the desire to harm herself and continue to do so until he is certain this is no longer an issue.

Self-injury and other self-destructive behaviours

During the first few months of therapy, self-injury, when already present, is difficult to prevent. The reason for this is that the patient has not yet developed alternatives for her tendency to punish herself or others and to suppress feelings. During this period, the therapist can make agreements with the patient in order to help prevent the most damaging of these behaviours, by replacing them with less damaging actions that have strong sensory stimulus (e.g. cold showers, holding ice cubes and running fast). The therapist can insist that the patient call him first before engaging in self-damaging activities. The therapist attempts to curtail other forms of self-destructive behaviour such as periodic drug abuse. In the case of serious drug addiction, sometimes the help of a detoxfication centre is necessary before ST can take place. In the end, this behaviour will be reduced as limited reparenting reduces the influence of the modes that are responsible for these behaviours. The therapist can teach the patient different ways of distracting herself or relaxing when faced with painful feelings (see Linehan, 1993). The therapist may have to resist using formal limit setting to control self-damaging behaviour, as it may be too early to win the battle. Often the therapist has to tolerate self-damaging behaviour, while continuously encouraging the patient to stop.

Suicide

When a patient is suicidal the therapist can temporarily increase the frequency of the sessions. This can be done either by adding an extra session or adding a few telephone sessions either at the discretion of the patient or planned. During these sessions, the therapist evaluates the cause(s) resulting in the patient's suicide attempts or desires, and offers her as much support as possible. If the patient agrees, he makes agreements with individuals in her surroundings who are prepared to care for her on a temporary basis. It is important that he avoids including family members in these agreements as they may be the source of the problem. Further, the therapist consults with colleagues and may consider temporarily medicating the patient. Should all of this prove unsuccessful, the therapist can organize a crisis hospitalization, either voluntary or involuntary. It is impossible to continue with therapy when the therapist is constantly worried about whether or not the patient will commit suicide. If the frequency of these suicide attempts, in spite of the extra efforts of the therapist and the co-therapist, does not decrease, it is necessary for him to set limits on this behaviour with his patient and, when necessary, organize hospitalization (see Chapter 4, 'Setting Limits'). By continual suicide threats, there is a very high risk that the therapist will overstep his own personal limitations and become discouraged with the therapeutic process and prematurely end treatment.

Trauma Processing

The processing of childhood traumas is an important part of ST. This takes place after the patient has achieved enough safe attachment to the therapist. Imagery rescripting is generally used in dealing with this problem. This method is also used earlier in therapy to investigate the origins of the different modes by using childhood experiences to trace the patient's dysfunctional interpretations and during the phase of changing dysfunctional schemas. Because of this, imagery rescripting will be a trusted method when it comes into use with trauma processing. If the patient does not bring up the trauma, the therapist should suggest this topic and ensure that it does not disappear from the agenda. This is a difficult phase of the therapy and timing is very important (just before the therapist's holidays would not be a good idea). The patient must also have a relatively stable living situation (i.e. not in the middle of moving or a divorce). Further she must have support from someone outside of the therapy sessions. Even when all of these conditions have been met, the patient may not want to deal with her childhood traumas. She needs an acceptable explanation as to why it is important for her to work through these traumas. The single most important reason is that her basic feelings of abandonment, inferiority and distrust are direct results of her childhood traumas. The constant reminders of these traumas serve to reinforce her dysfunctional schemas. In addition, the side effects from these traumas (e.g. nightmares and concentration problems) will continue to plague her until the traumas are properly dealt with.

The trauma treatment described here differs from imaginary exposure in the sense that the key feature is not exposure to the trauma memories, but rather the rescripting. In phase 1, memories of the moment just prior to when the actual trauma took place are recalled ("just before mother started to hit me with a stick"). And in phase 2 a timely intervention takes place ("mother's hand is pushed away and mother is put out of the room" = rescripting. In other words, the rescripting is what should have taken place at that time to protect the child). It is important that the dysfunctional, childlike interpretation ("I deserved to be hit because I was bad") changes into a functional interpretation ("I was not a bad child and no child deserves to be beaten with a stick because she makes a mistake"). It is recommended in the later phases of trauma-focused imagery rescripting that the patient should be encouraged to stand up for herself using her healthy adult mode. When she succeeds in stopping the violence or abuse, this will further reinforce the feeling that she is capable of solving her own problems. Once trauma-focused imagery rescripting is finished, the patient will need time to assemble her emotions and discuss the conclusions. Therefore, it is important to schedule enough time for this type of session. An imagery rescripting session is generally followed by a more cognitive directed session. The patient can complete her cognitive diary as a homework assignment, focusing on the topics of guilt and shame. The therapist can make himself available on the phone, outside of sessions, should the emotions become overwhelming once the patient has returned home. He does this to try and help avoid a crisis.

Problems with processing traumas

Patients experience very strong emotions during these sessions. Because of this it is necessary that the therapist is well versed in dealing with traumas and is able to deal with these strong emotions, as it is his job to support her during this process.

The therapist must take care not to suggest memories of events that did not take place. If the patient is unsure as to whether or not an event actually took place, the therapist must emphasize that whether an event is factual or not is not of the greatest importance here. For this method the focus is how the patient experienced this event (factual or not) and how the conclusions she drew, based on this, influenced the development of her dysfunctional schemas. The Dutch Society for Psychotherapy highly recommends that members do not use information obtained during such sessions against perpetrators in a legal sense.

In Chapters 4–8, various therapeutic methods and techniques used in ST were discussed. When possible, the appropriate phase of therapy and the mode for which the technique is intended was given for the different techniques. However, this is not sufficient to go by and treat the different modes in the most appropriate manner. Because of that, Chapter 9 discusses the techniques for each different mode separately.

9

Methods per Mode

Each mode demands a different, unique approach. Some of the previously mentioned techniques are better suited to certain modes than others. This is further complicated by the fact that the different modes are constantly interchanging with each other, both during sessions and out of sessions. One mode influences the other without the patient appearing to have any control over them. The therapist should try to name the modes he observes during sessions as they occur. Eventually the patient will also learn to differentiate between the different modes, both during and outside of sessions. Not all of the techniques we have described in Chapters 4–8 are recommended for use with all of the modes or during each phase of therapy. Because of this we describe which techniques in the field of feeling (experiential techniques), thinking (cognitive techniques) and doing (behavioural techniques) can be used with which mode and how to adapt the therapeutic attitude towards each mode. We have also included information about pharmacotherapy and which obstacles the therapist may face, while reacting to one of the modes. However, even this is not enough to adequately put this therapy into practice as the modes continually change requiring the therapist's attitudes and methods to also continually change as necessary. In the section 'A Simultaneous Chess Play in a Pinball Machine' later in this chapter, we describe how the therapist can best deal with the quick and constantly changing modes during therapeutic sessions.

Schema Therapy for Borderline Personality Disorder. Arnoud Arntz and Hannie van Genderen
© 2009 John Wiley & Sons, Ltd.

Treatment Methods for the Detached Protector

Therapeutic relationship

In the beginning of the therapy the therapist must often deal with the detached protector. The patient is frightened by the strong emotions of the abandoned or angry child. She also fears punishment and/or humiliation from the punitive parent. The therapist must regularly reassure the detached protector that he will support his patient when this happens and help her deal with these strong and often unpleasant emotions. He encourages her to express her emotions. He speaks to the detached protector in a friendly yet firm voice. During each session, the therapist must continually try to bypass the detached protector even if this takes a great deal of effort. While the patient is in her detached protector mode, it is not possible for the therapist to reach the abandoned child with limited reparenting (see Chapter 4). At times the protector can even become aggressive, often as a result of the patient not having enough trust in her therapist. Because of this, the protector is prepared to do, and does, anything and everything to ensure the therapist does not get near the abandoned child. The protector does this with the aim of protecting the patient from further abuse. This means that the therapist must have patience and continue to earn the patient's trust in him. If the patient is mistrusting, her therapist must make it clear that the fact that she does not trust him is evidence that she is in the protector mode and he must show understanding for her inability to trust. He must express empathy with her, let her know that learning to trust someone takes time, particularly if one has a past of putting their trust in untrustworthy individuals. The therapist can choose to increase the frequency and/or length of the sessions in trying to bypass the protector because usually the protector will back down in this situation. Outside of the session the protector can show their side by means of self-injury or suicide attempts. To an extent, physical pain protects the patient from emotional pain. In this case, all attention must first focus on putting an end to self-injury and/or suicide attempts. The therapist must ensure that he is easily accessible to the patient in this situation and that a crisis centre is available when he is not.

Feeling

The best method for removing the detached protector from the situation is the two-chair technique. The therapist asks the patient to sit in a different chair and from this new position put into words why the protector is needed. While in this other chair the patient can put her fears into words without immediately becoming emotional. Then, the therapist can have a discussion with the protector. During this discussion he emphasizes that the protector had a functional role in Little Nora's past when she was unable to escape her difficult situation. However, now Nora's situation has changed and she can allow Little Nora to be protected by the therapist and he will teach her how to handle emotions in another (more adult) way. When the relationship between therapist and patient is strong and trusting, the patient often becomes emotional by this reassurance and moves into the abandoned child mode. The therapist can then ask her to return to her original chair and continue the discussion with the abandoned child. When the protector agrees that the therapist continues with the abandoned child, he asks her to return to her chair even if she is not visibly emotional.

Another possibility is to avoid the protector all together by asking the patient to close her eyes and imagine Little Nora. If this is successful, then the therapist can try to reach the abandoned child in this manner and encourage her to express her feelings.

Thinking

The therapist can write down the pros and cons of the protector on a board. In practice, it is the patient who will think of pros and the therapist must help to find cons. He must explain why it is in her best interest to learn to deal with her feelings and emotions. This is an important skill for future intimate relationships and/or having children. Further it will help her with her general development as a person (see Table 9.1). This cognitive technique helps the patient to lessen the detached protector mode.

The other cognitive techniques described in Chapter 6 are less useful in this situation. This is because what appears to have changed on a cognitive level is often not assimilated at an emotional level. The new insights have not sunk in.

Doing

The patient must learn to spend less time in the protector mode both during sessions and outside of sessions. She can only be successful in doing this outside of sessions once she is able to do so during sessions. Further, the

Table 9.1   Examples of the pros and cons of the detached protector.

Pros	Cons
I feel quiet	I feel empty
I don't feel the urge to cut myself	If I suppress my feelings too long, I'll end up hurting myself
I don't have conflicts with other people	I don't connect with other people (or my therapist)
I don't have to talk about difficult issues in the session	I cannot start a new relationship when I stay detached
I don't have to try new things like working or studying	I don't learn how to handle emotions, so I should better not raise children. Otherwise they'll get the same problems as I have
	I don't learn how to overcome my problems
	If I don't find new work or a training course, I will never get a normal income
	If I stay in the detached protector mode, my life will be boring

patient also needs to have built up trust in others outside of the therapeutic framework. The therapist encourages her to share her feelings with others more and more often. If she has little contact with others, he can encourage her to participate in activities where she is likely to meet people regularly. Once she has developed relationships with a few good friends, it is helpful to invite them for one or more sessions to stimulate the patient by encouraging her to practise expressing her emotions towards them.

Pharmacotherapy

The use of psychopharmacology has been suggested if the patient's level of fear and panic reaches a point that she can no longer tolerate. Antidepressive drugs can be used in this case. However, there are at least two reasons to be extremely careful with the use of psychopharmics during ST. First, there are indications that pharmacological agents interfere with the emotional and cognitive change processes during treatment, so that recovery is delayed (Giesen-Bloo *et al.*, 2006). Secondly, their application might actually strengthen the detached protector mode, the opposite ST aims for. Should everything go well, after about a year the protector will be much less present. Further, the times that the protector is present, it will be much easier to set him on the sidelines.

Obstacles

- If the patient appears tired or sleepy, it is almost impossible to get through to her. The therapist must first find out if this is due to an actual lack of sleep and if so, which mode is responsible for her insomnia. Once this is established, the therapist and patient can work together to improve her sleep patterns. However, if there appears to be no physical explanation for her being tired, it is more than likely the result of the protector. In this case the therapist can try different methods to 'wake her up' such as opening a window, talking louder or even (gently) shaking her. Often it is helpful to begin with a difficult subject, which is more likely to force the patient to become more alert. When the patient's 'absence' begins to take the form of a dissociative state, the therapist can attempt to remove her from this state by means of concentration exercises such as controlled breathing, focusing on a certain point in the room, and having her describe where she is and with whom. He continues to reassure her that he will protect her from her punitive side. While doing this the therapist tries to discover what made the patient so frightened that she went into this dissociative state. He further tries to connect the results of this search to traumatic experiences from the patient's past.
- Large amounts of stress combined with serious fear can result in short-term psychotic symptoms. These psychotic symptoms often have a paranoid content. For example, the patient may think that her therapist is about to hit her or she sees him looking at her in an aggressive manner. In these situations it is as if the therapist becomes the abusive parent. Just as when a patient becomes dissociative, the therapist must also slowly, and in detail, reassure her and try to bring her back to reality when she shows psychotic symptoms. As the stress levels decrease, these psychotic symptoms will also decrease. The therapist need not worry about a full-blown psychotic episode based on these symptoms. Temporary use of antipsychotic drugs is sometimes indicated (the ability to counteract illusions is limited).
- At times the therapist does not know whether or not he is dealing with the protector as the patient makes apparently sensible statements while at the same time asking the therapist to come up with practical solutions

for her situation. He may think that he is dealing with the healthy adult. To clarify the situation the therapist can ask his patient about her feelings. If she appears to have a flat emotionless reaction, then he knows he is dealing with the protector. Looking for practical solutions while the patient is in the protector mode is seldom a good idea, as this mode is not focused on the needs of the young child. On the other hand, if she responds in a nuanced manner, then the therapist knows he is dealing with a healthy adult mode. Even when she is in the abandoned child mode, if the patient feels that she has enough support from the therapist it is possible for her to think of practical solutions herself without the protector.

Treatment Methods for the Abandoned and Abused Child

Therapeutic relationship

As discussed in detail in Chapter 4, building a trusting therapeutic relationship with the patient is a continuous point of interest from the start of therapy onwards. When the patient is in the abandoned child mode, the therapist can support and comfort her. Further he can help her discover different healthy options for meeting her needs while respecting the needs of others. It is not necessary to think up practical solutions for her problems at this point, but rather for the therapist to empathize with the feelings and rights of the patient. It is of particular importance for the therapist to be supportive in a warm and understanding manner. His patient should clearly hear this in the tone of his voice and mannerisms. During difficult periods in the patient's life, the therapist himself can either call her or allow her to call him between sessions as extra support. The purpose of this is also so that the patient learns to feel empathy for the little child she once was. As therapy progresses, the healthy adult mode will offer more and more of this needed support to the abandoned child. Because of this, the extra attention (e.g. between-session telephone calls) will become less necessary.

Feeling

Virtually all experiential techniques are helpful at this stage of therapy to allow the abandoned child the opportunity to express her feelings. These techniques, in particular imagery rescripting and historical role play, also show her that it is perfectly normal to ask for and receive help and support when one is dealing with difficult situations. Later in therapy she will learn to integrate this attitude into her healthy adult mode and will not require the therapist's support as often. To encourage this, it is good to stimulate the patient to play the role of the healthy adult, who takes care of the abandoned child in imagery rescripting. For most BPD patients this is not possible until the final phase of therapy. When patients were forced by circumstances to take over the role of parent(s) during their childhood, the therapist must take care not to expect the patient to take the role of healthy adult too early in therapy. The patient must first have a period during which she can be a child and experience the care of the therapist before growing up and becoming a healthy adult. In historical role play, the third phase, in which she must try out different behaviours, will be the most difficult as she will have to think of alternative behaviours that she does not yet possess because her personal experience is very limited. The therapist can help by modelling options before the patient herself tries them.

Thinking

By using cognitive techniques the patient can learn what a normal childhood involves. She can incorporate details she missed out on during her own childhood as well as learn how to fulfil her needs in the future. The patient can read about general childhood development to increase her understanding of normal development. Furthermore, the therapist can suggest that she learns about the universal rights of children to get an idea of what normal standards actually are. The therapist can make flashcards or recordings in which he says positive things about the patient and asks her to read or listen to these at home. One of the most important mistakes the patient makes when she is in the abandoned child mode is concluding that simply because things happened in a certain way, they will always happen in this way. She has an inadequate perspective of time. The concept of (very bad) things becoming less painful over time can help her become less anxious and sad.

Doing

The therapist shows the patient that he appreciates her by speaking in a friendly and respectful manner to her. He also regularly praises her to show his recognition of her as a person as well as her efforts to learn how to do things in a different manner. The patient must also learn to give herself compliments.

Sometimes it is necessary for a patient to temporarily break off contact with her parents or other individuals who have a damaging influence on her life. This is especially necessary if the parents continue to respond to the patient in the same manner as when she was a child. In this case it is best to limit contact to a minimum until the patient has developed an adequately strong healthy adult mode. Once she has done this she can decide for herself whether or not she wants to retain contact with her parent(s) and in which way. Limiting contact, even briefly, is very difficult for the patient. She often feels frightened she will be plagued by feelings of guilt (punitive) or end up feeling even more alone in the world (abandoned). She will trivialize the so-called bad influence of her parent(s) and may even become angry with her therapist (protector). Where there was 'only' emotional abuse or neglect, instead of physical or sexual abuse, the patient will be particularly reluctant to reduce contact with the parents. The therapist must therefore be cautious when dealing with this topic and discuss both the pros and cons. This requires a strong, safe therapeutic relationship and possibly the therapist making extra time for the patient. An important catalyst for a temporary break in contact with the parents is often that despite having two sessions a week, therapy is not progressing due to the daily negative influence of the parents.

As described in the section on the protector, the patient can practise sharing her feelings and asking for and receiving support from new contacts. Relaxation and meditative exercises are also a way of learning to accept the unpleasant feelings of the abandoned child.

Obstacles

- The therapist can become too good a parent. Too much extra care for the patient can result in the therapist overstepping the boundaries of the therapeutic relationship. Young *et al.* (2003) defines the boundaries for the therapist as follows: "The therapist has no contact with the patient outside of the work relationship and does not make the patient too dependent upon him or satisfy his own needs via the patient. This is about 'limited' reparenting not actual parenthood."
- The therapist can set himself too far away from the role of a parent and find the patient's behaviour childish. He must be willing and able to accept at least part of the patient's problems as from a young child who

does not have the ability to deal with these problems on her own. The therapist must be willing to put extra energy and time into treatment. He must see the patient not as greedy, but rather as someone who is in need of certain things. In doing so, he must find a balance between 'too much' and 'too little' in regard to fulfilling her needs. It is helpful for the therapist to tell the patient that her needs are normal and he understands them but cannot always be 100% ready to meet them immediately or in an adequate manner. By doing so, he does not disregard these needs or insist that the patient repress her emotions (something the punitive parent would do). On the other hand, requiring her to wait increases her frustration tolerance by teaching her that her needs cannot always be met exactly when she wants them to be.

Treatment Methods for the Angry/Impulsive Child

Therapeutic relationship

The angry child requires a safe therapeutic relationship in which clear boundaries are set by the therapist (see Chapter 4, 'Setting Limits'). Within these boundaries the angry child should be able to express her anger (see Chapter 5, 'Anger') and also learn appropriate assertiveness (see Chapter 7, 'Skills Training and Role Play'). This entire topic of anger is usually faced later on in therapy, as the patient does not dare to express these emotions early in therapy out of fear of the punitive parent or rejection by the therapist. At times, the patient is so frightened of her own aggression that she does not show up for the session at all. In this case the therapist can call her at the time she should have had her session and discuss her fears with her. He can try to reassure her that he will not be shocked or punish her when she becomes angry, but rather help her express her anger. If the patient fears becoming uncontrollable and accidentally hurting the therapist, they can agree that if she loses control, she can temporarily leave the room only returning once her rage has diminished. A better method is to show her how to vent her anger by, for example, hitting a pillow. The therapist demonstrates this by actually physically hitting a pillow and shouting. In doing so he encourages her to do the same, always keeping a pillow close at hand should her anger flare up. In this way the patient gets the message that anger, no matter how strong, is acceptable. However, the expression of this anger must take place in a non-damaging manner. This allows many patients enough security to express their anger more and more often.

Feeling

If the patient is unable to get in touch with her feelings of anger, it is the job of the therapist to help her (see Chapter 5, 'Anger'). When using imagery rescripting situations from the patient's past, in which she was very angry but was not able to do anything about this anger, the therapist makes sure that the punitive parent cannot harm the patient. He can do this by, for example, creating an unbreakable see-through wall or bars separating the angry child from the punitive parent. Another possible solution is that he ties up or holds back the punitive parent. By doing this he gives the angry child or healthy adult the opportunity to express her anger. If she is unable to do so, the therapist can also do this for her. He can physically show anger (e.g. hitting a pillow) and encourage her to do so with him.

After this type of imagery exercise it is important to discuss an emergency plan with the patient and decide on different alternatives for dealing with the punitive parent should it return and seek revenge outside of the sessions. Sometimes, soon after participating in this type of exercise, the patient will feel the need to hurt herself or possibly attempt suicide as punishment for expressing her angry emotions. Should this threaten to happen, the patient can call her therapist or other health care workers. If, however, the therapist has doubts about her ability to actively call for help, he can 'check up' on her by making telephone appointments and asking how she is doing during these calls.

Thinking

BPD patients often have a number of irrational thoughts surrounding feeling and/or expressing anger. These irrational thoughts are excellent material for treatment with cognitive therapy. Observing how ordinary individuals deal with anger is helpful in building an understanding of how to express anger in a normal way.

Doing

First the patient must practise expressing mild irritations and anger during sessions and later outside of the sessions (also see Chapter 7, 'Skills Training and Role Play'). This can take the form of an experiment in combination with challenging dysfunctional thoughts. If she appears to have problems with anger and restlessness at home and cannot directly place where this anger comes from, it is likely to be residual anger from her past which is not yet ready to be processed. Physical activity is helpful in curbing this unrest. Some patients find hitting a pillow or boxing bag helpful while others use sports as a form of release. While one patient may prefer using sports to release this anger, another patient might frantically clean the house. The therapist can use the following session to explore aspects that elicited this rage.

Pharmacotherapy

Anger leads to insomnia in some patients. Occasional use of benzodiazepines can help break this cycle as the patient runs the risk of exhaustion, and when she is overly tired her ability to deal with the punitive parent mode is compromised. However, in most cases the use of benzodiazepines is not recommended as they have the side effect of unbridling the patient and can actually increase the chances of uncontrollable fits of rage. Antihistamines may be a better alternative as sleep medication.

Obstacles

- One should not underestimate the risk of the presence of the punitive parent, particularly once the session is completed. The therapist must never forget to talk about this possibility at the end of a session in which the angry child was present.
- The angry child can evoke more negative reactions from the therapist than the other modes. Because of this, the therapist must take care to keep his own reactions under control particularly when the angry child's aggression is directed towards him. He must do his best to view the patient as a child in the middle of a tantrum, stomping her foot in anger. Should he not succeed in controlling his own anger and respond to her attack with a counter-attack, the patient will no doubt begin to feel rejected (abandoned child). Another risk is that the therapist wants to pull away from the patient because he cannot stand her anger. This is not to say that the therapist should not set limits to the patient's aggressive behaviour. While he must tolerate her *feeling* angry, he need not tolerate all forms of expressing this anger. In doing so he does not reject her anger, but rather discusses with her which part of it is realistic and what is unrealistic. On the other hand, if the therapist actually does

become frightened of his patient, he must investigate whether he is dealing with an angry child or an angry protector. In either case, he must ensure that the necessary boundaries and limitations are clear in order for him to feel safe again.

- Angry Nora can also turn towards self-injury and suicide as a way of showing anger. In this mode she does not intend to punish herself, but to take revenge on those around her who have unjustly hurt her. In rare cases the patient may also threaten to kill these individuals who have wronged her. When a patient threatens suicide and/or murder, the therapist is put under an enormous strain and must again set very clear boundaries and enlist the involvement of a colleague (see Chapter 8, 'Suicide and Self-Injury').

Treatment Methods for the Punitive Parent

Therapeutic relationship

The therapist protects the patient as much as possible from the punitive parent mode. This mode is very dangerous because the fact that the patient wants to punish herself can lead to destructive behaviour such as self-injury and suicide. During therapy the therapist tries to create as safe a situation as possible and makes sure that he is reachable in the event of a crisis (see Chapter 8, 'Crisis' and 'Suicide and Self-Injury'). Despite all of his efforts, the patient will at times interpret comments from the therapist as punitive. Most often the therapist is not aware of this; however, when the patient suddenly changes from one mode to another (to the punitive parent or protector), there is a large chance that the therapist said something 'wrong'. He can ask the patient if this is the case and try to explain what he actually meant by his comments. It is possible, however, that the therapist did indeed react in a punishing way. This is most probably due to falling into the trap of acting out negative counter-transference and he must repair this situation. The therapist is the role model of a good parent (who also makes mistakes at times) and takes a completely opposite stance to that of the punitive parent.

Feeling

In imagery rescripting the therapist combats the punitive parent and teaches the patient to fight against this punishing mode. This can also be achieved using historical role play. The multiple-chair technique is an excellent method for dealing with the punitive parent (see Chapter 5). A hard confrontational manner is the best method for dealing with a punitive parent whose behaviour towards the patient is clearly cruel and derogatory. The therapist talks in a louder voice and interrupts the punitive parent should he refuse to listen. He uses a more formal type of language in dealing with the punitive parent by referring to him or her as Mr or Mrs X (name of parents). When the punitive parent is critical in a negative sense towards the patient, the accent of the disputation should lie in pointing out the parent's own failings and rigidity. The critical parent appears reasonable and only stops when the parent's own shortcomings are pointed out. One aspect he has definitely failed at is raising his daughter in a loving and accepting way. This is a particularly helpful method if this critical side is connected to one of the parents. The therapist, who should have enough information about this parent, gathered during intake interviews, can offer convincing examples.

Another possible variation on this theme is that of the guilt-inducing, complaining parent. This type of punitive parent insists that all attention be focused on him/her and holds Little Nora responsible for the parent's unhappiness. Should Nora attempt to go her own way, she is punished and reproached. The patient herself finds her parent pitiful and feels responsible for the parent's happiness, and therefore cannot directly disagree with the parent. In this case the therapist is not very strict with the punitive mode, but is more resolute in dealing with it. He tells the punitive mode that he must seek help for himself and must not rely on Little Nora to solve his problems.

As with all experiential techniques, the therapist should not start an extended discussion with the punitive side, because doing so would only be an admission that the punitive side is partially correct. The punitive parent is not a person who is capable of thinking in a nuanced manner, but rather a mode that will attack even the slightest faults and mistakes. Thinking about things in a distinctive, refined manner is part of a healthy adult's schema, not that of a punitive parent.

Thinking

When the patient has negative thoughts about herself and realizes that this is due to the punitive mode, she can try to make a balanced judgement of herself using a cognitive diary with the help of her healthy adult side. The punitive parent will judge the patient in a very black-and-white manner. Thoughts like "I am evil, dumb and ugly and everything is my fault" are common. Techniques that can be used in this situation are multidimensional evaluation, the pie chart and the courthouse method (see Chapter 6). In addition the patient can ask other people who are close to her for help and advice by asking them for their point of view on, for example, a mistake that she has made.

Keeping a positive logbook and historical testing are other methods that provide arguments opposing the punitive parent mode.

Developing healthy adult norms and values is also a way to reduce the influence of the punitive parent as the patient is afraid that no norms and values will be left if she lets go of the excessively strict standards of her parents. The therapist should help her to develop more flexible and more reasonable norms without forcing his own ideas upon her. These new values and norms belong to the healthy adult.

Doing

The patient can do a number of things to rid herself of the punitive parent mode, for example:

- Listen to a recording during which the therapist sends the punitive parent away.
- Read through flashcards with statements as to why the punitive parent is incorrect.
- Visit friends and ask for support and affection.
- Relax using meditative or relaxation exercises.
- Do things that the patient enjoys doing or is good at.
- Learning to comfort herself, if necessary using a transitional object.
- Have a schema dialogue at home between healthy and punishing modes.

For further information about these forms of homework, please refer to Chapter 8, 'Homework'.

Obstacles

- The punitive parent can return after a session in which he was silenced and seek revenge. The therapist must not underestimate this. Different measures for dealing with this situation have been described earlier in this chapter under 'Treatment Methods for the Angry/Impulsive Child'.

- The punishing side sometimes causes the patient not to do what is good or healthy for her, but rather to do the complete opposite. This comes from the thought that she does not deserve to be happy. It is also an unconscious attempt to provoke punishment from her therapist. This often leads to the patient not showing up for sessions. In this case the therapist must call the patient and convince her that he will not punish her, even though things have gone wrong. Further he must encourage her to attend the next session. If the patient is not available on the telephone, the therapist should send her a letter in which he expresses his concern for her well-being and invites her to the next session.

- The patient can also become protective of her parents ("they couldn't help it; they had bad childhoods themselves"). The therapist explains that it is important to silence the punitive parent as this mode is damaging for the patient. He repeats that by rejecting the punitive parent, the patient is not rejecting the parent as he or she is now, but rather that part of the parent that was not good and was punishing during the patient's youth. Actual understanding the parent or forgiveness only takes place once therapy has been completed and becomes the choice of the patient as a healthy adult. The patient must first learn to silence the punitive parent mode in her own head.

Treatment Methods for the Healthy Adult

Therapeutic relationship

The therapeutic relationship changes slowly but surely from that of a parent–child relationship to that of a relationship between two adults. The patient becomes more and more autonomous and is able to find solutions to her problems without the help of the therapist. From the very beginning of therapy the therapist searches for contact with the healthy adult, even if these moments are few and far between. In particular when dealing with aggressive and impulsive behaviour, the therapist seeks contact with the healthy adult directly and tries to end this behaviour in order to continue with therapy.

Example of talking with the healthy adult

Nora is threatening to stop therapy because her boyfriend broke up with her and now life has no meaning.

T: Nora, I understand that you're having a very difficult time right now but I want to talk to your healthy adult side. What I want to say is that you shouldn't stop therapy now because you will end up having more problems. I understand that right now you feel like it's going nowhere, but you also felt this way when we began therapy but you stuck it out. Right now everything may seem hopeless, but your healthy adult knows that this will pass and I can help you with it.

Feeling

The patient is capable of expressing and sharing her feelings with others. This is easily observed during therapy sessions as her feelings are expressed without any deterrents. The stories she shares with the therapist show her ability to deal with emotions and feelings in her relationships with others. When she is faced with strong emotions, she is capable of researching which one of her old schemas is at work. She can offer alternative healthy schemas to counter these old schemas on her own.

Thinking

The healthy adult is capable of studying the underlying thoughts of threatening negative feelings or impulsive behaviour and disputing them. She can think about herself and the world as a whole in a nuanced manner and is competent in having a Socratic dialogue (see Chapter 6) in her head without having to write everything down in a cognitive diary.

Doing

The patient participates in different sorts of activities appropriate to a normal adult lifestyle such as maintaining friendships and building a relationship. She either works or studies or has some other meaningful way to fill her days. The healthy adult makes the final decisions as to those individuals from her past she wishes to maintain contact with and those she chooses not to.

Obstacles

During the first half of the therapy the therapist may sometimes think he is talking to the healthy adult while in reality he is being faced by the protector. Especially when dealing with patients whose protector has a strong tendency to rationalize and trivialize, the therapist can be led to believe that the pathology he is dealing with is not too serious. In this phase the therapist has to ask himself whether this healthy behaviour is in accordance with the severity of the pathology at the start of therapy. He has to at least check the emotions of the patient to get more clarity on this issue (see earlier discussion on obstacles when dealing with the protector).

A Simultaneous Chess Play in a Pinball Machine

In short, the therapist is meant to support the abandoned child, teach the angry child to express her rage in an appropriate manner, make the protector's role unnecessary, send the punitive parent away, and help the healthy adult develop and flourish. We have described per mode just how the therapist can go about achieving these goals. This systematic description suggests that in using this therapy it is possible to plan which mode one is going to work on during a given session. Unfortunately this is not the case in actual practice. Just as the patient herself has no control over her modes, neither does the therapist. The modes pop up and switch off constantly in no particular order. At times the patient feels like the ball in a pinball machine, being constantly pushed around by others (the flippers) into different, unexpected or undesired places. Each new place the ball is shot off to represents yet another different mode for the patient. The actions of the therapist are aimed at creating calmness in this pinball machine until the patient herself learns to control where she wants the ball to go using her healthy adult mode. Each time a new mode pops up during a session, it is up to the therapist to research this change, name the present mode and modify his therapeutic strategy. If he waits too long in doing this, he runs the risk of his efforts having no therapeutic value as well as deterioration of the therapeutic relationship or in a worst-case scenario, the patient stopping therapy altogether.

Example of reactions to quickly changing modes

Nora arrives frightened (abandoned child). She has just seen an acquaintance with whom she broke off contact in the past after they had an argument.

T: (friendly) I see that you have had quite a shock. That makes perfect sense seeing as you had not expected to see him.
P: I don't dare leave this office; maybe he's waiting for me.
T: (reassuring) Are you afraid that he will try and hurt you? It was many years ago, don't you think it won't be that bad?
P: (feels the therapist thinks she is exaggerating) No you're right, I'm exaggerating again and making too big of a deal out of the whole thing (punitive parent).
T: (is not immediately aware that this is the punitive parent) I don't think you're exaggerating, but I wonder if after so many years he's still got something against you.
P: No it's true, I don't need to make such a big deal out of this. Let's talk about something else (protector).

The remainder of the session is spent discussing another topic. It seems as though this was a reasonable conversation with a healthy adult. However, just under the surface, there is the recurring theme of the patient's fear for this old acquaintance. She does not dare bring this subject up with her therapist for fear of rejection, and at the end of the session this fear reappears.

P: Despite all of this, I still don't know whether or not I'll make it home in one piece. You can't help me (abandoned child).
T: (immediately becomes defensive = his own pitfall failure) Oh, I thought you didn't want to talk about that anymore.
P: (the protector is activated and says): Well maybe therapy doesn't help in this kind of situation. I was thinking about stopping therapy altogether.
T: This is indeed a good topic to discuss in therapy and we can start off with it during the next session.

End of session

Because the therapist took too long to realize that he was dealing with the abandoned child, the protector was activated. Now the therapist runs the risk of losing his connection with the abandoned child. Should the patient not show up for her next session, it is very important that the therapist makes all attempts to contact her and acknowledge his mistake and convince her to continue with therapy.

What complicates this situation is the fact that the modes are overlapping. While the one mode is actively present, the others are constantly lurking in the background. Because of this, all the modes hear what the therapist says. At times the various modes react (in silence) to what the therapist says and the patient experiences this as a sort of 'war' or chaos in her head. From the therapist's point of view it is as if he is playing chess blindfolded with five (or more) players. Each player (mode) makes his moves on a separate board. It is then up to the therapist to keep all of the different boards in the back of his head and remember which player's turn it is.

Example of dealing with different modes during one single intervention

Nora enters the session in the punitive parent mode and begins speaking about herself in a negative manner.

P: I'm such a failure, I can't even begin that assignment. It's due in a week and I haven't even started!
T: (friendly) If I am hearing you correctly, I hear the punitive parent talking about you in a negative way.
P: Of course after so many failures.
T: I suggest that we set aside another chair for this mode so that I can say something to it because I don't agree at all.

(patient nods and both of them look at the empty chair, the place for the punitive parent)

T: (in a clearly harsher voice) I don't think Nora is a failure at all. And you're not helping by talking to her like this, you're just making things worse. If you continue, then she will start drinking again and then become a mess. So stop it right now, then I can talk with Little Nora and find out what happened.

At the moment, the therapist is playing on the punitive parent's board. He then sets this mode in another chair and tells it to be quiet. At the same time, and on the boards of the protector and the abandoned child, the therapist also passes on a message to them.

To the protector he says: "If this continues, then you will become active again and Nora will start drinking."

To the abandoned child, he says: "I want to help you, so I am telling the punitive parent to stop and the protector to stay away."

If all goes well, Little Nora will immediately feel the therapist's support. Should he succeed in silencing the punitive parent for the remainder of the session, then Little Nora can continue to talk to the therapist and he can continue to support her and help her solve her problem. If all of this is going as planned, then the protector will hear this on its own separate board and realize that it is not needed at this time.

When playing chess blindfolded it is eminent that sometimes the player (the therapist) will win, sometimes he will lose and sometimes it will end in a draw. In ST the therapist must not lose his match against the punitive parent because then he loses the matches with the other modes as well. When this happens, the abandoned child's board is filled with fear and sadness, the angry child's board is filled with rage, while the protector's board senses that something is not right and grows stronger. Playing chess in the dark like this is often a game of hit and miss for the therapist. The therapist must develop a talent so as not to fall into his own traps (modes). Should this appear to be happening, he must take the time to analyse this with a colleague and then continue where he left off. Surprisingly enough it is often possible to analyse what went wrong together with the patient. Both he and the patient can agree to recognize this situation sooner should it arise again. In short, BPD is so complicated that in addition to vast knowledge and skills, the therapist must also remain patient, be flexible and possess the ability to put things into proper perspective. Good, regular peer supervision is therefore absolutely indispensable.

10

Final Phase of Therapy

Behavioural Pattern-Breaking

Once the schema modes are no longer actively present, there may still be remnants of schemas and/or coping styles that must be dealt with. "Even if patients have insight into their Early Maladaptive Schemas, and even if they have done the cognitive and experiential work, their schemas will reassert themselves if patients do not change their behavioural patterns" (Young, Klosko and Weishaar, 2003, p. 146). The manner in which the patient manages her schemas must be tackled. For example, Nora had the tendency to put difficult things off by rationalizing that these things were not that important. For descriptions of schemas and coping styles please refer to Appendices I and J.

Together with her therapist, the patient makes a list of behaviours that still need to be altered and puts them in order of importance. Included in this list are also important decisions she still has to make, such as choices regarding education or employment. If she avoids mentioning an important subject, the therapist can press her to add this to the list.

During this phase the therapist can make more use of empathetic confrontation to encourage her to finish this last part of the therapy. He encourages her to observe the advantages and disadvantages of the last changes she has to make during this last phase of therapy. Practising new behaviours and doing homework becomes more important in this final phase of the therapy than it has previously been (see Appendix H). The two-or-more-chair technique and imagery rescripting can be used to help elicit changes in patterns of behaviour (see Chapter 5).

Schema Therapy for Borderline Personality Disorder. Arnoud Arntz and Hannie van Genderen
© 2009 John Wiley & Sons, Ltd.

Ending Therapy

The last phase of therapy often involves some kind of mourning process as the patient must accept the fact that her parents will not change and that she will not be able to return to childhood and experience the things she missed from them. The patient searches to find a new, mostly less intensive, relationship with her parents and with other family members.

The patient will also slowly begin to let go of her therapist and begin to stand on her own feet. The frequency of sessions is reduced. As the therapist has been the only person she could trust in her life for a long time, this process is not easy for her and requires a great deal of effort. The patient's fear of abandonment will arise again and has to be dealt with. Because the therapist also has a strong bond with his patient, this process of saying goodbye may also be difficult for him. The therapist must take care to offer his patient the space and the trust to move on on her own. He does this in the same way that a parent would when his child grows up and moves on. Patients often continue to maintain contact with their therapist particularly when important events occur in their lives (e.g. wedding, birth of a child, or a difficult event like death of a parent or a relationship crisis). In general, the therapist responds with a card. When the patient experiences serious difficulties, she might return to the therapist for help. Usually, a few booster sessions suffice. In line with the limited parenting concept, it is important that the bond between patient and therapist remains, even when treatment is formally stopped.

According to Young, therapy is only finished when the patient has found a good (healthy for her) partner (Young, personal comments to author). In one study we nevertheless observed successful cases who did not (yet) have an intimate partner.

11

Conclusion

Until recently, many therapists were convinced that the only achievable goal for BPD patients was a bit of stability in their lives. The therapy we have described in this book looks like yielding much better results than a simple, stable life. In many patients, significant and serious changes in their personalities appear to take place. In the study by Giesen-Bloo *et al.* (2006) it appeared that 52% of patients no longer met the criteria for BPD upon completion of ST, and almost 70% improved reliably. These individuals have satisfying relationships with others and are capable of regular employment or have found other meaningful activities to fill their days. What remains unclear from research is exactly which patients are more likely to benefit from ST and which are not, although patients using medication had a much lower chance of recovery.

There is a perception that individuals who have had BPD in the past will retain a certain amount of vulnerability regarding situations that are similar to their childhood traumas (e.g. loss of a partner). A recent brain imaging study indicated that recovered BPD patients have normalized emotional responses. Nevertheless, there may remain (latent) vulnerabilities in these patients. The clinical impression in the situation of a need for help is that a few sessions are enough to help the former BPD patient get back on track. It is important that the patient receives help from her own former therapist during this crisis. He knows her well and it will be easier for him to identify which schemas have become active and reassure her. He is also well aware of how she overcame her problems in the past and knows which healthy coping strategies are most likely to work for her and helps her to activate

Schema Therapy for Borderline Personality Disorder. Arnoud Arntz and Hannie van Genderen
© 2009 John Wiley & Sons, Ltd.

these strategies. Future scientific research must investigate which factors play a role in possible relapse.

Experience has shown that therapists using ST tend to find working with BPD patients enjoyable. They develop a better understanding of their patients and experience more possibilities to help them. This is not to say that this is easy work and that a therapist can start helping 10 different BPD patients at the same time using this method. The maximum number should remain somewhere between four or five patients who have progressed to the point where the most problematic aspects are dealt with. The use of ST in a group setting is still in development, but may prove to further expand the possibilities for treating BPD.

Appendix A

Brochure for Patients: Schema Therapy for People with Borderline Personality Disorder

What Is Borderline Personality Disorder?

People with borderline personality disorder (BPD) have problems with mood swings. They experience problems in almost every aspect of their lives because of these mood swings, particularly in their relationships. Often they do not know who they are or what they want. These individuals also have a tendency to act in very impulsive ways. They often experience outbursts of anger/rage and crises are not uncommon. Individuals with BPD do not know why their moods swing in this uncontrollable manner. Molehills quickly become mountains and the result is often frightening or makes them angry. While many people with BPD are intelligent and creative, they are seldom able to succeed in developing these talents. Often their education remains incomplete and they work far below their abilities. They run the risk of hurting themselves. Research has shown that the suicide risk in this group is higher than in other personality disorders. Further, in an attempt to numb overpowering emotions, these individuals often abuse various substances (e.g. drugs and/or alcohol).

What Is Schema Therapy?

Schema therapy is a form of therapy that involves a combination of cognitive behavioural therapy and elements from other types of therapy. These

Schema Therapy for Borderline Personality Disorder. Arnoud Arntz and Hannie van Genderen
© 2009 John Wiley & Sons, Ltd.

are all directed not only at the current problems the patient is experiencing but also at assessing the patient's past and the sources of these problems.

Description of BPD from the Perspective of Schema Therapy

Schema Therapy assumes that people developed ideas about themselves, the others and the world around them during their childhood. These ideas have taught people how to deal with the different situations that they experience as an adult. If during your childhood you had virtually no support or direction, in other words were emotionally neglected, it would have been impossible to learn important information about yourself, others and the world around you. If one adds to this emotional, physical and/or sexual abuse, the chance is even greater that normal development is disrupted. The result is that you do not experience yourself as a whole, because you have developed different sides of yourself and they appear to express themselves at different times. These different sides are referred to as schema modes or schema states. Most individuals with BPD have five schema modes: the abandoned/abused child, the angry child, the punitive parent, the protector and the healthy adult. People with BPD have two modes that are characteristic of their childhood abuse and/or neglect. These schema modes express a behaviour that is childlike with very strong, often uncontrollable emotions and absolute ideas. The other three modes have to do with more adult characteristics. The punitive side and the protector, while appearing to be helpful, are not helping at all as their presence interferes with the development of the healthy adult.

The abandoned and abused child

When you are in this mode, you feel abandoned, helpless, frightened and threatened. You think that at any given moment terrible things will happen. There is no one you can trust and there is no possibility for help.

The angry child

If you are so angry that you lose control of yourself, then the angry child is active. You feel that you have been unfairly treated and wronged so that direct frontal attack is the best defence. You may also be very impulsive in wanting to satisfy your wants and needs as a rebellion against an unjust world.

The punitive side

This side puts the opinions of one (or more) of your childhood caregivers who mistreated you into words. The punitive side does not approve of showing emotions and thinks that you deserve to be punished for all of your mistakes, even accidents. This side gives you the feeling that you are bad, dumb, lazy and ugly. At times these feelings can be so strong that you may feel you should not even exist. The punitive side directs itself against all of the child modes.

The detached protector

Both the child sides as well as the punitive side carry along with them very strong emotions, which can at times be unbearable. The protector helps you to avoid these feelings. Sometimes this makes you feel empty or 'nothing'. At other times substances (drugs, alcohol) are abused to push these feelings away. The detached protector shuts you off from others so that no one can hurt you.

The healthy adult

This side can handle emotions and solve problems well. But as many things in your childhood have gone wrong, you have not sufficiently developed this side and it is often not present when you need it most.

Goal of Schema Therapy

The goal of schema therapy is to strengthen the healthy adult and teach the child sides to deal with intense emotions without being scared of an outburst of rage. The punitive side is not needed any more and will be replaced with normal, nuanced values and norms. The detached protector is gradually less necessary as the punitive side disappears and you are not suddenly overcome by your feelings any more.

What does the therapy consist of?

The therapy consists of a number of different ways to accomplish the aforementioned goal.

Relationship with the therapist

The therapist helps you learn the things you could not learn in your childhood.

The therapist tries to support and understand you instead of punishing you so that you learn to trust a person. Since this trust was destroyed to a great extent in your childhood, this is an important experience.

Experiential techniques

The experience and expression of emotions was suppressed and dealt with in a disturbed way. The therapist can, for instance, ask you to close your eyes and go back to the situations in the past. He asks you what you actually would have wanted to happen at that time, and he helps you to express your needs (in your imagination) and to stop the maltreatment. This way you learn that your emotions and needs were normal, but the reactions to them were not.

Cognitive techniques

Cognitive therapy is concerned with the thoughts and ideas about yourself, the others and the world, which have degenerated through the negative experiences in your childhood and the rest of your life. Evidence for and against this way of thinking will be looked for. In case there are many contradictory arguments, the therapist can propose a debate between the two viewpoints, in which you defend one position and the therapist defends the other. Then, the roles are switched and you try to defend the contrasting opinion. This way you acquire more nuanced perspectives.

Behavioural techniques

Not only your emotions and thought must be changed, but also what you do as a result. Behavioural techniques usually consist of exercises to try out a new behaviour. If, for instance, you have never learned to express your opinion, you practise this skill first with the therapist and later in situations outside of therapy.

What you can expect

A combination of the described techniques will lead to a more positive image of yourself, teach you who you can and cannot trust, and the best way of tackling problems. The different sides of you will cooperate more and you develop into a healthy adult. Since the problems have been there for a long time and your development is disturbed in many ways, this therapy will ask a lot of you and take at least two to three years. Try to talk about problems with your therapist by following and persevering with the therapy so that you will eventually be much better.

Appendix B

Cognitive Logbook for Modes

ACTIVATING EVENT (What caused my reaction?)
FEELING (How did I feel?)
THOUGHT (What was I thinking?)
BEHAVIOUR (What did I do?)
THE FIVE ASPECTS OF MYSELF Which aspect was in play in this situation? Underline the aspects you recognize and describe them. 1. Detached protector: 2. Abandoned/Abused child: 3. Angry/Impulsive child: 4. Punishing parent: 5. Healthy adult:

Schema Therapy for Borderline Personality Disorder. Arnoud Arntz and Hannie van Genderen
© 2009 John Wiley & Sons, Ltd.

JUSTIFIED REACTION (What part of my reaction was justified?)

OVERREACTION (What part of my reaction was too strong?)

In which way did I overreact or see things that were not there?

What did the different aspects of myself do to make things worse?

DESIRED REACTION

What would be a better way for me to view this situation and to deal with it?

What could I do to solve this problem in a better manner?

FEELING

Appendix C

Positive Logbook

Try to write down one or more small (or large) activities or experiences that contribute towards a positive image of yourself and others. All of this information can be used to weaken the punitive mode and strengthen the healthy adult mode.
Date: Subject:
Date: Subject:
Date: Subject:
Date: Subject:
Date: Subject:
Date: Subject:
Date: Subject:

Schema Therapy for Borderline Personality Disorder. Arnoud Arntz and Hannie van Genderen
© 2009 John Wiley & Sons, Ltd.

Appendix D

Historical Testing

Write down experiences that took place in the different phases of your life that prove that the punitive parent is wrong and that support the little child.
0–2 years
3–5 years
6–12 years
13–18 years
19–25 years
26–35 years
36–50 years and older
Summary:

Schema Therapy for Borderline Personality Disorder. Arnoud Arntz and Hannie van Genderen
© 2009 John Wiley & Sons, Ltd.

Appendix E

Experiments

Instructions for the therapist

Planning an experiment:

1. Decide with the patient whether or not it is useful to find out if an idea is tenable.
2. A theory can only be tested if it is falsifiable.
3. If desired, formulate alternative theories.
4. Together with the patient, decide upon a concrete situation in the near future, in which the idea is likely to play a role.
5. Together with the patient, decide upon concrete behaviours that clearly test the idea (i.e. which can lead to falsification).
6. Allow the patient to predict where the behaviours from no. 5 are likely to lead to, based upon the to-be-tested idea.
7. Beforehand, agree upon which concrete results, based on the aforementioned behaviours, will serve as evidence for or against the accuracy of the idea.
8. Beforehand, agree upon where and when the patient will try out these new behaviours and exactly what she must pay attention to. One should expect a great deal of fear regarding her anticipation of this exercise.
9. Remember this is an experiment and an experiment cannot fail!

Schema Therapy for Borderline Personality Disorder. Arnoud Arntz and Hannie van Genderen
© 2009 John Wiley & Sons, Ltd.

Evaluation of the experiment:

1. Do not forget: an experiment cannot fail! However, it is possible that it was not executed, wrongly executed or wrongly designed.
2. Allow the patient to blow off steam after this exercise and empathize with the courage she has shown by attempting to execute it.
3. Ask the patient to retell the situation, behaviour and concrete consequences of the experiment.
4. Based upon the concrete results of the experiment, discuss whether or not the predictions were correct. Be careful to avoid misinterpretations.
5. Summarize the results and, together with the patient, re-evaluate the tested idea.

Pitfalls:
1. Essential components of the new behaviour were not executed.
2. The experiment cannot offer a decisive answer to the idea.
3. The idea is incorrectly formulated and does not accurately represent the patient's theories.
4. The patient rejects the results. Search for the reasons and watch out for misinterpretations. Invite the patient to set up a decisive test.
5. The therapist got too involved in a specific outcome of the experiment.

Date:
The original thought to be tested for credibility
The alternative thought to be tested for credibility

Behavioural experiment: What am I going to do and how am I going to do it?

Which results support the original thought?

Which results support the alternative thought?

Result: How did the behavioural experiment go?
Which results appeared to support the original thought and which appeared to support the alternative thought?

Credibility of the original thought:

Credibility of the alternative thought:

What have I learned from this experiment?

Which mode has changed because of this and how has it changed?

Appendix F

Homework Form

Description of the homework assignment I want to do:
When will I do this homework assignment?
What potential problems can I think of when it comes to doing this assignment? 1. 2. 3.
Possible solutions to these problems: 1. 2. 3.
Results:
Effects on the modes:
Which problems appeared that I did not think of beforehand and how did I deal with them?

Schema Therapy for Borderline Personality Disorder. Arnoud Arntz and Hannie van Genderen
© 2009 John Wiley & Sons, Ltd.

Appendix G

Problem Solving

What is the problem?	
What do I want to achieve?	
Which modes are likely to interfere with my solving this problem? 1. 2.	
Which thoughts are likely to interfere with my solving this problem? 1. 2.	
What alternative thoughts help me to solve this problem? 1. 2.	

Schema Therapy for Borderline Personality Disorder. Arnoud Arntz and Hannie van Genderen
© 2009 John Wiley & Sons, Ltd.

What solutions can I think of for this problem?
1.
2.
3.
4.
5.
6.

List pros and cons for each solution

Which of these solutions do I choose and why?

How did I deal with it?

What was the result and did I achieve my goal?

What influence did the result have on the modes?

Eventually: Which other solution will I try?

Result:

Appendix H

Changing Behavioural Patterns

Description of the behavioural pattern I want to work on:
In what kind of situations does this behaviour often appear?
What do I do in these situations that results in things not going well?
Which mode, rule of life or thought plays an important role here?
What are the arguments against this mode, rule of life or thought?
What is a new behaviour that would be more goal-orientated in this situation?
How did it work out when I tried out this new behaviour?
Formulate a new and healthier rule of life:

Schema Therapy for Borderline Personality Disorder. Arnoud Arntz and Hannie van Genderen
© 2009 John Wiley & Sons, Ltd.

Appendix I

Eighteen Schemas (Young *et al.*, 2003)

In this appendix the 18 schemas as described and summarized by Young, Klosko and Weishaar (2003) are listed and described briefly. We refer to this book for a detailed explanation on the meaning of the schemas and schema therapy. In accordance with Young *et al.*, this appendix will refer to the patient in the feminine form and refer to the therapist using the masculine form. The 18 schemas are organized in five themes, shortly introduced before the schemas are described.

Disconnection and Rejection

The patient expects that she cannot rely on the security or predictability of her surroundings. Further she assumes a lack of reliability, support, empathy and respect from others. She comes from a family in which she was treated in a cold, rejecting manner. She was lonely and had no emotional support; at times she even lacked basic care. Her parents (caregivers) were unpredictable, uninterested or abusive.

1. Abandonment/instability

The patient expects that she will soon lose anyone with whom she has an emotional attachment. She believes that all of her intimate relationships will eventually end. Important others in her environment are seen as

Schema Therapy for Borderline Personality Disorder. Arnoud Arntz and Hannie van Genderen
© 2009 John Wiley & Sons, Ltd.

unreliable and unpredictable in their ability or willingness to support her or in their devotion to her. They will either die or abandon her. In either case, she will end up alone.

2. Mistrust/abuse

The patient is convinced that others will, in one way or another, eventually take advantage of her. She expects others to purposely hurt her, cheat on her, manipulate and/or humiliate her. She believes that she will always have the short end of the stick.

3. Emotional deprivation

The patient thinks that her primary emotional needs are either not met or inadequately met by others. These needs are related to physical care, empathy, affection, protection, companionship and care. The most common forms of emotional deprivation are as follows:

– *Deprivation of Nurturance:* No attention, warmth or companionship
– *Deprivation of Empathy:* No one listens to you, understands you or can share your feelings.
– *Deprivation of Protection:* No one gives you advice or direction.

4. Defectiveness/shame

The patient feels that she is intrinsically incomplete and bad. As soon as others get to know her better, they will also discover this and no longer want anything to do with her. She thinks that no one will find her worthy of loving. She is overly concerned with the judgement of others and is very conscious of herself and her inadequacies. These feelings of being incomplete and inadequate often result in strong feelings of shame. Defectiveness/shame can be related to both inner ('negative' desires and needs) and outer (undesirable physical appearance or being socially inadequate) aspects of the self.

5. Social isolation/alienation

The patient has the feeling that she is isolated from the rest of the world, is different from everyone else and does not fit in anywhere.

Impaired Autonomy and Performance

The patient expects that she is incapable of functioning and performing on her own and independently of others. She comes from a (clinging) family from which she cannot break free and in which she is overly protected.

6. Dependence/incompetence

The patient is not capable of taking on daily responsibilities and cannot do so independently. She feels extremely dependent upon others in situations that require her to make decisions on simple daily problems or to attempt anything new. She appears completely helpless.

7. Vulnerability to harm or illness

The patient is convinced that at any given moment, something terrible could happen to her and that there is absolutely nothing she can do to protect herself from this impending disaster. She fears both medical and psychological catastrophes as well as other types of adversity. She takes extraordinary precautions to avoid disasters.

8. Enmeshment/undeveloped self

The patient is overly involved with and connected to one or more of her caregivers. Because of this over-involvement she is unable to develop her own identity. At times the patient has the idea that she does not exist without the other person and often feels empty and without goals.

9. Failure

The patient is convinced that she is not capable of performing at the same level as her peers with regard to career, education or sport. She feels stupid, foolish, talentless and ignorant. She does not even attempt to succeed at things as she is convinced she will be unable to do so successfully.

Impaired Limits

The patient has inadequate boundaries, feelings of responsibility and frustration tolerance. She is not good at setting realistic long-term goals and has difficulty working together with others. She comes from a family that offered little direction or gave the feeling of being superior to the rest of the world. The parents set few limitations and did not encourage the patient to persevere during difficult times and/or take others into consideration.

10. Entitlement/grandiosity

The patient thinks that she is superior to others and has special, only-for-her rights. She does not need to follow the 'normal' rules as she is above them. She can do and get away with what she wants without taking others into consideration. The main theme here is power and control over situations and individuals. There is no empathy for others.

11. Insufficient self-control/self-discipline

The patient cannot tolerate any frustration in achieving her goals. She is not capable of suppressing feelings or impulses. It is possible that she is primarily attempting to avoid unpleasantness or being uncomfortable (pain, argument and effort).

Other-Directedness

The patient always takes the needs of others into consideration and suppresses her own needs. She does this in order to receive love and approval from others. She comes from a family that only accepted her given certain conditions. The needs and status of the parents took priority over the individual character of the child.

12. Subjugation

The patient gives herself over to the will of others to avoid negative consequences. This can include the suppression of all her needs or emotions. The patient thinks that her desires, opinions and feelings are not cared for by others. This often leads to pent-up rage, which is then expressed in an inadequate manner (i.e. passive–aggressive or via psychosomatic symptoms). One can distinguish between subjugation of needs and subjugation of emotions, but they usually go together.

13. Self-sacrifice

The patient voluntarily and regularly sacrifices her needs for others whom she views as weaker than herself. If she does attend to her own needs, she feels guilty about doing so. She is overly sensitive to the pain of others. Because her own needs are not met she eventually resents those she cares for.

14. Approval-seeking/recognition-seeking

The patient searches for approval, appreciation and acknowledgement in an exaggerated manner. She does this at the cost of her own development and needs. This sometimes results in an excessive desire for status, beauty and social approval in order to achieve acknowledgement and admiration.

Overvigilance and Inhibition

At the cost of self-expression and relaxation, the patient suppresses her spontaneous feelings and needs and follows her own set of strict rules and values. The patient's family emphasized achievement, perfectionism, and repression of feelings and emotions. The caregivers were critical, pessimistic and moralistic while at the same time expecting an almost unachievable high standard.

15. Negativity/pessimism

The patient always sees the negative side of things while she ignores or minimizes the positive side. Eventually, everything will go wrong even if it is currently going well. Because she is convinced that everything will eventually go wrong, she is constantly worried and hyper-alert. She often complains and does not dare to make any decisions.

16. Emotional inhibition

The patient always holds in her emotions and impulses as she thinks that expressing these will damage others or lead to feelings of shame, abandonment or loss of self-worth. This involves suppressing all spontaneous expression: anger, joy, as well as discussing problems. She emphasizes rationalization.

17. Unrelenting standards/hypercriticalness

The patient believes that she will never be good enough and that she must always try harder. She tries to satisfy an unusually high set of personal standards to avoid criticism. She is critical of herself as well as of others around her. This results in perfectionism, rigid rules, and a preoccupation with time and efficiency. She does this at the cost of enjoying herself, relaxing and maintaining social contacts.

18. *Punitiveness*

The patient feels that individuals should be severely punished for their mistakes. She is aggressive, intolerant and impatient. She is completely unforgiving of mistakes. She does not take an individual's circumstances or feelings into account.

Appendix J

Coping Strategies

Coping strategies are mechanisms for dealing with schemas. All organisms have three manners of dealing with threat: freeze, flight and fight. When confronted with a schema, an individual can react in any one of these ways.

In this appendix we will describe briefly the three ways in which one can cope with schemas, as described in detail by Young, Klosko and Weishaar (2003) to which we refer the reader for further reading.

Surrender (Schema-Affirming Behaviour: *Freeze*)

The patient behaves in accordance with her schema and adapts her thoughts and feelings accordingly. This behaviour confirms the schema.

Behaviour: Approving and dependent.
Thoughts: Selective information processing, in other words, only information that supports the presence of the schema is of importance.
Feelings: The emotional pain from the schema is directly felt.

Schema Therapy for Borderline Personality Disorder. Arnoud Arntz and Hannie van Genderen
© 2009 John Wiley & Sons, Ltd.

Avoidance (Schema-Evasive Behaviour: *Flight*)

The patient avoids activities that trigger the schema and the accompanying feelings. The result is that the schema is not questioned and therefore no corrective experiences can take place.

Behaviour: Active and passive avoidance of all kinds of situations that could potentially activate the schema.
Thoughts: Denial of situations and memories; depersonalization.
Feelings: Denial or levelling off of feelings (includes self-injury and substance abuse).

Overcompensation (Showing the Opposite Behaviour in Order to Fight the Schema: *Fight*)

The patient behaves completely opposite to her schema to avoid having problems from it. This results in the patient underestimating the influence of her schema and often in overly assertive or independent behaviour.

Behaviour: The pitfall of overly exaggerating the opposing behaviour.
Thoughts: Denial that this schema is applicable for the patient.
Feelings: The patient covers up unpleasant schema-related feelings with opposing feelings (e.g. power as a cover-up for powerlessness or pride as a cover-up for inferiority). However, the unpleasant feelings return when the overcompensation fails due to setbacks or illness.

References

Adams, H.E., Bernat, J.A. and Luscher, K.A. (2001) Borderline personality disorder: an overview, in *Comprehensive Handbook of Psychopathology*, 3rd edn (eds P.B. Sutker and H.E. Adams), Kluwer Academic/Plenum Publishers, New York.

American Psychiatric Association (APA) (2000) *Diagnostic and Statistical Manual of Mental Disorders Text Revision (DSM-IV-TR)*, 4th edn, American Psychiatric Association, Washington, DC.

Arntz, A. (1999) Do personality disorders exist? On the validity of the concept and its cognitive-behavioural formulation and treatment. *Behaviour Research and Therapy*, **37**, 97–134.

Arntz, A. (2004) Borderline personality disorder, in *Cognitive Therapy of Personality Disorders*, 2nd edn (eds A.T. Beck, A. Freeman, D.D. Davis and Associates), Guilford, New York, pp. 187–215.

Arntz, A. and Bögels, B. (2000) *Schemagerichte Cognitieve Therapie voor Persoonlijkheidsstoornissen, Praktijkreeks Gedragstherapie*, Bohn Stafleu Van Loghum, Houten, the Netherlands.

Arntz, A. and Dreessen, L. (1995) BPD checklist. Maastricht University, internal document.

Arntz, A., Dreessen, L., Schouten, E. and Weertman, A. (2004) Beliefs in personality disorders: a test with the personality disorder belief questionnaire. *Behaviour Research and Therapy*, **42**, 1215–25.

Arntz, A. and Kuipers, H. (1998) Cognitieve gedragstherapie bij de borderline persoonlijkheidsstoornis, in *Behandelingsstrategieën bij De borderline persoonlijkheidsstoornis* (eds W. van Tilburg, W. van den Brink and A. Arntz), Bohn Stafleu Van Loghum, Houten, the Netherlands, pp. 42–64.

Arntz, A. and Weertman, A. (1999) Treatment of childhood memories: theory and practice. *Behaviour Research and Therapy*, **37**, 715–40.

Arntz, A., van den Hoorn, M., Cornelis, J. *et al.* (2003) Reliability and validity of the borderline personality disorder severity index. *Journal of Personality Disorders*, **17**, 45–59.

Asselt, A.D. van, Dirksen, C.D., Arntz, A., Giesen-Bloo, J.H., Dyck, R. van, Spinhoven, P., Tilburg, W. van, Kremers, I.P., Nadort, M. and Severens, J.L. (2008) Outpatient psychotherapy for borderline personality disorder: lost-effectiveness of schema-focused therapy vs. transference-focused psychotherapy. *British Journal of Psychiatry*, **92**, 450–7.

Ball, S.A. and Cecero, J.J. (2001) Addicted patients with personality disorders: traits, schemas, and presenting problems. *Journal of Personality Disorders*, **15**, 72–83.

Beck, A.T., Freeman, A., Davis, D.D. and Associates (2004) *Cognitive Therapy of Personality Disorders*, Guilford Press, New York.

Beck, A.T. (2002) *Cognitive Therapy of Borderline Personality Disorder and Attempted Suicide*. Paper presented at the 1st annual conference of the Treatment and Research Advancements Association for Personality Disorders, December 2002, Bethesda, MD.

Beck, J.S. (1995) *Cognitive Therapy: Basics and Beyond*, Guilford, New York.

Brown, G.K., Newman, C.F., Charlesworth, S.E. *et al.* (2004) An open clinical trial of cognitive therapy for borderline personality disorder. *Journal of Personality Disorders*, **18**, 257–71.

Burns, D.D. and Auerbach, A. (1996) Therapeutic empathy in cognitive-behavioral therapy: does it really make a difference? in *Frontiers of Cognitive Therapy* (ed. P.M. Salkovskis), Guilford, New York, p. 135.

Butler, A.C., Brown, G.K., Beck, A.T. and Grisham, J.R. (2002) Assessment of dysfunctional beliefs in borderline personality disorder. *Behaviour Research and Therapy*, **40**,1231–40.

Dreessen, L. and Arntz, A. (1998) The impact of personality disorders on treatment outcome of anxiety disorders: best-evidence synthesis. *Behaviour Research and Therapy*, **36**, 483–504.

Giesen-Bloo, J., Arntz, A. and Schouten, E. (2008) Reliability and validity of the Borderline Personality Disorder checklist. (submitted)

Giesen-Bloo, J., van Dyck, R., Spinhoven, P., van Tilburg, W., Dirksen, C., van Asselt, T., Kremers, I., Nadort, M. and Arntz, A. (2006) Outpatient psycho-therapy for borderline personality disorder: randomised trial of schema-focused therapy vs transference-focused psychotherapy. *Archives of General Psychiatry*, **63**, 649–58.

Giesen-Bloo, J., Wachters, L., Arntz, A. and Schouten, E. (2008) Assessment of borderline personality disorder with the Borderline Personality Disorder Severity Index-IV: psychometric evaluation and dimensional structure. (submitted)

Herman, J.L., Perry, J.C. and van der Kolk, B.A. (1989) Childhood trauma in bor-derline personality disorder. *American Journal of Psychiatry*, **146**, 490–5.

van IJzendoorn, M.H., Schuengel, C. and Bakermans-Kranenburg, M.J. (1999) Disorganized attachment in early childhood: meta-analysis of precursors, concomitants, and sequelae. *Development and Psychopathology*, **11**, 225–49.

Kernberg, O.F. (1976) *Object Relations Theory and Clinical Psycho-Analysis*, Jason Aronson, New York.

Kernberg, O.F. (1996) A psychoanalytic theory of personality disorders, in *Major Theories of Personality Disorder* (eds J.F. Clarkin and M.F. Lenzeweger), Guilford, New York, pp. 106–37.

Kernberg, O.F., Selzer, M.A., Koenigsberg, H.W. *et al.* (1989) *Psychodynamic Psychotherapy of Borderline Patients*, Basic Books, New York.

Layden, M.A., Newman, C.F., Freeman, A. and Morse, S.B. (1993) *Cognitive Therapy of Borderline Personality Disorder*, Allyn & Bacon, Boston.

Linehan, M.M. (1993) *Cognitive-Behavioral Treatment of Borderline Personality Disorder*, Guilford, New York/London.

Linehan, M.M., Armstrong, H.E., Suarez, A. *et al.* (1991) Cognitive-behavioral treatment of chronically parasuicidal borderline patients. *Archives of General Psychiatry*, **48**, 1060–4.

Lobbestael, J., van Vreeswijk, M.F. and Arntz, A. (2008) An empirical test of schema mode conceptualization in personality disorders. *Behaviour Research and Therapy*, **46**, 854–60.

McGinn, L.K. and Young, J.E. (1996) Schema-focused therapy, in *Frontiers of Cognitive Therapy* (ed. P.M. Salkovskis), Guilford, New York, pp. 182–207.

Mulder, R.T. (2002) Personality pathology and treatment outcome in major depression: a review. *American Journal of Psychiatry*, **159**, 359–71.

Nordahl, H.M. and Nysæter, T.F.P.E. (2005) Schema therapy for patients with borderline personality disorder: a single case series. *Journal of Behavior Therapy and Experimental Psychiatry*, **36**, 254–64.

Ogata, S.N., Silk, K.R., Goodrich, S. *et al.* (1990) Childhood sexual and physical abuse in adult patients with borderline personality disorder. *American Journal of Psychiatry*, **147**, 1008–13.

van Oppen, P. and Arntz, A. (1994) Cognitive therapy for obsessive-compulsive disorder. *Behaviour Research and Therapy*, **32**, 79–87.

Padesky, C.A. (1994) Schema change processes in cognitive therapy. Clinical *Psychology and Psychotherapy*, **1**, 267–78.

Paris, J. (1993) The treatment of borderline personality disorder in light of the research on its long-term outcome. *Canadian Journal of Psychiatry*, **38** (Suppl. 1), 28–34.

Simpson, E.B., Yen, S., Costello, E. *et al.* (2004) Combined dialectical behavior therapy and fluoxetine in the treatment of borderline personality disorder. *Journal of Clinical Psychiatry*, **65**, 379–85.

Sprey, A. (2002) *Praktijkboek persoonlijkheidsstoornissen, Diagnostiek, cognitieve gedragstherapie en therapeutische relatie*, Bohn Stafleu Van Loghum, Houten, the Netherlands.

Stoffers, J., Lieb, K., Voellm, B. *et al.* (2008) Pharmacotherapy of BPD. Cochrane Library. (in preparation)

Weaver, T.L. and Clum, G.A. (1993) Early family environment and traumatic experiences associated with borderline personality disorder. *Journal of Consulting and Clinical Psychology*, **61**, 1068–75.

Weertman, A.M., Arntz, A., Schouten, E. and Dreessen, L. (2005) Influences of beliefs and personality disorders on treatment outcome in anxiety patients. *Journal of Consulting and Clinical Psychology*, **73**, 936–44.

Young, J. (1999) *Cognitive Therapy for Personality Disorders: A Schema Focused Approach*, Professional Resource Exchange, Sarasota, FL.

Young, J.E. and Klosko, J.S. (1994) *Reinventing Your Life*, Plume, New York.

Young, J.E., Klosko, J.S. and Weishaar, M.E. (2003) *Schema Therapy: A Practitioner's Guide*, Guilford, New York.

Zanarini, M.C. (2000) Childhood experiences associated with the development of borderline personality disorder. *The Psychiatric Clinics of North America*, **23**, 89–101.

Further Reading

Arntz, A. (2008) Schema-focused therapy for borderline personality disorder: effectiveness and cost-effectiveness, evidence from a multicenter trial. *European Psychiatry*, **23** (Suppl. 2), S65–S66.

Arntz, A. and Bernstein, D. (2006) Can personality disorders be changed? *Netherlands Journal of Psychology*, **62**, 9–18.

Arntz, A. and Bögels, S. (2000) *Schemagerichte cognitieve therapie voor persoonlijkheidsstoornissen. [Schema-focused cognitive therapy for personality disorders]*. Houten: Bohn Stafleu van Loghum.

Arntz, A., Klokman, J. and Sieswerda, S. (2005) An experimental test of the schema mode model of borderline personality disorder. *Journal of Behavior Therapy and Experimental Psychiatry*, **36**(3), 226–39.

Arntz, A., Tiesema, M. and Kindt, M. (2007) Treatment of PTSD: a comparison of imaginal exposure with and without imagery rescripting. *Journal of Behavior Therapy and Experimental Psychiatry*, **38**, 345–70.

Arntz, A. and Weertman, A. (1999) Treatment of childhood memories: theory and practice. *Behaviour Research and Therapy*, **37**, 715–40.

Ball, J., Mitchell, P., Malhi, G., Skillecorn, A. and Smith, M. (2003) Schema-focused cognitive therapy for bipolar disorder: reducing vulnerability to relapse through attitudinal change. *Australian and New Zealand Journal of Psychiatry*, **37**(1), 41–8.

Ball, S.A. (1998) Manualised treatment for substance abusers with personality disorders: dual focus schema therapy. *Addictive Behaviours*, **23**, 883–91.

Ball, S.A. (2004) Treatment of personality disorders with co-occurring substance dependence: dual-focus schema therapy. In: J.J. Magnavita (Ed.), *Handbook of personality disorders: theory and practice* (pp. 398–425). Hoboken, NJ.: Wiley.

Ball, S.A. and Cecero, J.J. (2001) Addicted patients with personality disorders: traits, schemas, and presenting problems. *Journal of Personality Disorders*, **15**, 72–83.

Ball, S.A. and Young, J.E. (2000) Dual focus schema therapy for personality disorders and substance dependence: case study results. *Cognitive and Behavioural Practice*, **7**, 270–81.

Bamber, M. (2004) 'The good, the bad and defenceless Jimmy' – a single case study of schema mode therapy. *Clinical Psychology and Psychotherapy*, **11**, 425–38.

Bernstein, D.P., Arntz, A. and De Vos, M. (2007) Schema focused therapy in forensic settings: theoretical model and recommendations for best clinical practice. *International Journal of Forensic Mental Health*, **6**, 169–83.

Calvete, E., Esthc)vez, A., López de Arroyabe, E. and Ruiz, P. (2005) The Schema Questionnaire – short form: structure and relationship with automatic thoughts and symptoms of affective disorders. *European Journal of Psychological Assessment*, **21**(2), 90–9.

Cecero, J.J. and Young, J.E. (2001) Case of Silvia: a schema-focused approach. *Journal of Psychotherapy Integration*, **11**, 217–29.

Giesen-Bloo, J., Van Dyck, R., Spinhoven, P., Van Tilburg, W., Dirksen, C., Van Asselt, T. et al. (2006) Outpatient psychotherapy for borderline personality disorder: randomised clinical trial of schema-focused therapy vs. transference-focused psychotherapy. *Archives of General Psychiatry*, **63**, 649–58.

Gude, T. and Hoffart, A. (2008) Change in interpersonal problems after cognitive agoraphobia and schema-focused therapy versus psychodynamic treatment as usual of inpatients with agoraphobia and Cluster C personality disorders.

Gude, T., Monsen, J.T. and Hoffart, A. (2001) Schemas, affect consciousness, and Cluster C personality pathology: a prospective one-year follow-up study of patients in a schema-focused short-term treatment program. *Psychotherapy Research*, **11**(1), 85–98.

Hoffart, A. and Sexton, H. (2002) The role of optimism in the process of schema-focused cognitive therapy of personality problems. *Behaviour Research and Therapy*, **40**, 611–23.

Hoffart, A., Sexton, H. and Nordahl, H.M. (2005) Connection between patient and therapist and therapist's competence in schema-focused therapy of personality problems. *Psychotherapy Research*, **15**, 409–19.

Hoffart, A., Versland, S. and Sexton, H. (2004) Self-understanding, empathy, guided discovery, and schema belief in schema-focused cognitive therapy of personality problems: a process-outcome study. *Cognitive Therapy and Research*, **26**, 199–219.

Holmes, E.A., Arntz, A. and Smucker, M.R. (2007) Imagery rescripting in cognitive behaviour therapy: images, treatment techniques and outcomes. *Journal of Behavior Therapy and Experimental Psychiatry*, **38**, 297–305.

James, I.A. (2001) Schema therapy: the next generation, but should it carry a health warning? *Behavioural and Cognitive Psychotherapy*, **29**, 401–7.

Jovey, M. and Jackson, H.J. (2004) Early maladaptive schemas in personality disordered individuals. *Journal of Personality Disorders*, **18**, 467–78.

Kellogg, S.H. and Young, J.E. (2006) Schema therapy for borderline personality disorder. *Journal of Clinical Psychology*, **62**, 445–58.

Kennerley, H. (1996) Cognitive therapy of dissociative symptoms associated with trauma. *British Journal of Clinical Psychology*, **35**, 325–40.

Kremers, I.P., Van Giezen, A.E., Van der Does, A.J., Van Dyck, R. and Spinhoven, P. (2007) Memory of childhood trauma before and after long-term psychological treatment of borderline personality disorder. *Journal of Behavior Therapy and Experimental Psychiatry*, **38**(1), 1–10.

Lee, C.W., Taylor, G. and Dunn, J. (1999) Factor structure of the Schema Questionnaire in a large clinical sample. *Cognitive Therapy and Research*, **23**, 441–51.

Lobbestael, J., Arntz, A. and Sieswerda, S. (2005) Schema modes and childhood abuse in borderline and antisocial personality disorder. *Journal of Behavior Therapy and Experimental Psychiatry*, **36**(3), 240–53.

Lobbestael, J., Van Vreeswijk, M.F. and Arntz, A. (2007) Shedding light on schema modes: a clarification of the mode concept and its current research status. *Netherlands Journal of Psychology*, **63**(03), 76–85.

Lobbestael, J., Van Vreeswijk, M.F. and Arntz, A. (2008) An empirical test of schema mode conceptualisations in personality disorders. *Behaviour Research and Therapy*, **46**, 854–60.

Lobbestael, J., Van Vreeswijk, M.F., Spinhoven, P., Schouten, E. and Arntz, A. (submitted for publication). The reliability and validity of the Schema Mode Inventory (SMI).

Lundh, L. and Czyzykow-Czarnocka, S. (2001) Priming of the Emotional Stroop effect by a Schema Questionnaire. An experimental study of test order. *Cognitive Therapy and Research*, **25**, 281–9.

McGinn, L.K. and Young, J.E. (1997) Schema-focused therapy. In: P.M. Salkovskis (Ed.), *Frontiers of cognitive therapy* (pp. 182–207). New York: Guildford Publications.

Morrison, N. (2000) Schema-focused cognitive therapy for complex long-standing problems: a single-case study. *Behavioural and Cognitive Psychotherapy*, **28**, 269–83.

Nordahl, H.M. and Nysaeter, T.E. (2005) Schema therapy for patients with borderline personality disorder: a single case series. *Journal of Behavior Therapy and Experimental Psychiatry*, **36**(3), 254–64.

Padesky, C.A. (1994) Schema change processes in cognitive therapy. *Clinical Psychology and Psychotherapy*, **1**, 267–78.

Petrocelli, J.V., Glaser, B.A., Calhoun, G.B. and Campbell, L.F. (2001) Early maladaptive schemas of personality disorder subtypes. *Journal of Personality Disorders*, **15**, 546–59.

Ratto, C.L. and Capitano, D.L. (1999) New directions for cognitive therapy: a schema-focused approach. *Cognitive and Behavioural Practice*, **6**(1), 68–73.

Rijkeboer, M.M., Van den Bergh, H. and Van Den Bout, J. (2005) Stability and discriminative power of the Young Schema Questionnaire in a Dutch clinical versus non-clinical population. *Journal of Behavior Therapy and Experimental Psychiatry*, **36**(2), 129–44.

Schmidt, N.B., Joiner Jr., T.E., Young, J.E. and Telch, M.J. (1995) The schema questionnaire: Investigation of psychometric properties and the hierarchical structure of a measure of maladaptive schemas. *Cognitive Therapy and Research*, **19**, 295–321.

Sieswerda, S., Arntz, A. and Kindt, M. (2007) Successful psychotherapy reduces hypervigilance in Borderline Personality Disorder. *Behavioural and Cognitive Psychotherapy*, **35**, 387–402.

Smucker, M.R. and Niederee, J. (1995) Treating incest-related PTSD and patho-genic schemas through imaginal exposure and rescripting. *Cognitive and Behavioural Practice*, **2**(1), 63–92.

Spinhoven, P., Giesen-Bloo, J., Van Dyck, R. and Arntz, A. (2008) Can assessors and therapists predict the outcome of long-term psychotherapy in borderline personality disorder? *Journal of Clinical Psychology*, **64**, 667–86.

Spinhoven, P., Van Dyck, R., Giesen-Bloo, J., Kooiman, K. and Arntz, A. (2007) The therapeutic alliance in schema-focused therapy and transference-focused psychotherapy for borderline personality disorder. *Journal of Consulting and Clinical Psychology*, **75**, 104–15.

Stallard, P. (2007) Early maladaptive schemas in children: stability and differences between a community and a clinic referred sample. *Clinical Psychology and Psychotherapy*, **14**, 10–18.

Stallard, P. and Rayner, H. (2005) The development and preliminary evaluation of a Schema Questionnaire for Children (SQC). *Behavioural and Cognitive Psychotherapy*, **33**, 217–24.

Stopa, L., Thorne, P., Waters, A. and Preston, J. (2001) Are the short and long forms of the Young Schema Questionnaire comparable and how well does each version predict psychopathology scores? *Journal of Cognitive Psychotherapy*, **15**, 253–72.

Stopa, L. and Walters, A. (2005) The effect of mood on responses to the Young schema questionnaire: short form. *Psychological Psychotherapy*, **78**, 45–57.

Van Asselt, A.D., Dirksen, C.D., Arntz, A., Giesen-Bloo, J.H., Van Dyck, R., Spinhoven, P., et al. (2008) Out-patient psychotherapy for borderline per-sonality disorder: cost-effectiveness of schema-focused therapy v. transference-focused psychotherapy. *British Journal of Psychiatry*, **192**, 450–7.

Waller, G., Meyer, C. and Ohanian, V. (2001) Psychometric properties of the long and short versions of the Young Schema Questionnaire: core beliefs among bulimic and comparison women. *Cognitive Therapy and Research*, **25**, 137–47.

Waller, G., Shah, R., Ohanian, V. and Elliot, P. (2001) Core beliefs in bulimia nervosa and depression: the discriminant validity of Young's Schema Questionnaire. *Behaviour Therapy*, **32**(1), 139–53.

Weertman, A. and Arntz, A. (2007) Effectiveness of treatment of childhood memories in cognitive therapy for personality disorders: a controlled study contrasting methods focusing on the present and methods focusing on childhood memories. *Behaviour Research and Therapy*, **45**, 2133–43.

Welburn, K., Coristine, M., Dagg, P., Pontefract, A. and Jordan, S. (2002) The Schema Questionnaire – short form: factor analysis and relationship between schemas and symptoms. *Cognitive Therapy and Research*, **26**, 519–30.

Young, J.E. (1999) *Cognitive therapy for personality disorders: a schema-focused approach (revised edition)*. Sarasota, FL.: Professional Resource Press.

Young, J.E. (2002) Schema-focused therapy for personality disorders. In: G. Simos (Ed.), *Cognitive behaviour therapy* (pp. 201–222). New York: Routledge.

Young, J.E. (2005) Schema-focused cognitive therapy and the case of Ms. S. *Journal of Psychotherapy Integration*, **15**(1), 115–26.

Young, J.E., Arntz, A., Atkinson, T., Lobbestael, J., Weishaar, M. E., Van Vreeswijk, M., et al. (2007) *The Schema Mode Inventory*. New York: Schema Therapy Institute.

Young, J.E. and Flanagan, C. (1998) Schema-focused therapy for narcissistic patients. In: E.F. Ronningstam (Ed.), *Disorders of narcissism: diagnostic, clinical, and empirical implications* (pp. 239–268). Washington, D.C.: American Psychiatric Press.

Young, J.E. and Klosko, J.S. (1994) *Reinventing your life*. New York: Plume Books.

Young, J.E., Klosko, J.S. and Weishaar, M. (2003) *Schema therapy: a practitioner's guide*. New York: Guildford Publications.

Young, J.E. and Lindemann, M. (2002) An integrative schema-focused model for personality disorders. In: R.L. Leahy and E.T. Dowd (Eds.), *Clinical advances in cognitive psychotherapy: theory and application* (pp. 93–109). New York: Springer Publishing.

Index